D1269283

Wildlife in North America: Mammals

Wildlife in North America: Mammals

R. D. Lawrence

MICHAEL JOSEPH
LONDON

© R. D. Lawrence 1974

Published in Canada by Thomas Nelson & Sons (Canada) Limited,
81 Curlew Drive, Don Mills, Ontario, M3A 2R1.

Published simultaneously in the United States of America
by Chilton Book Company, Chilton Way, Radnor, Pennsylvania
19089, and in Great Britain by Michael Joseph Limited,
62 Bedford Square, London WC1B 3ES.

ISBN 0 7181 1354 3

Library of Congress Catalog Card Number 74-82664

Printed and bound in Canada

1234567890MR83210987654

To Mary Robson,
in appreciation of her help
and guidance in editing this book

Contents

9 Preface

11 Babes in the Woods — Opossum

15 The Tunnelers — Shrews—Moles

23 Inventor of Radar — Bats

28 The Toothless One — Nine-banded Armadillo

32 Eater of Trees — Porcupine

38 The Tree Dwellers — Flying Squirrel—Red Squirrel

46 The Sleepers — Chipmunk—Groundhog

54 Season of Plenty — Beaver

61 Mother Mouse — White-footed Mouse

66 A Creature of Water — Muskrat

73 Extra Teeth — Rabbits—Hares—Pikas

81 This Machine Will Self-Destruct — Snowshoe Hare—Lemmings

88 The Howling Pack — Timber Wolf

93 The Night Raiders — Coyote

99 Cunning Hunter — Red Fox

106 Giant of the North — Polar Bear

114 The Legend — Grizzly Bear

119 Birth of a Miracle — Black Bear

125 Old Coon's Tale — Raccoon

130 Coon Cousins — Ringtail—Coatimundi

136 Treetop Marauders — Pine Marten—Fisher

144 The Brown Savage — Mink

150 Matilda — Striped Skunk

156 Savage Fangs — Wolverine

161 Happy Bandits — River Otter

167 His Ninth Life — Lynx

174 The Hungry Night — Bobcat

178 Three-Toes — Cougar

185 Curious Cats — Ocelot—Jaguarundi

191 The Pig That Barks — Collared Peccary

194 Giant of the Forest — Moose

201 His Last Battle — Elk

209 The Swift Ones   White-tailed Deer
218 Herds of the Tundra   Barren-ground Caribou
225 The Swiftest Ones   Pronghorn
231 Monarch of the Plains   American Bison
235 From Another Age   Musk-Ox
241 The Lordly Ones   Rocky Mountain Bighorn
247 Frozen Peaks   Mountain Goat
254 Photo Credits
255 Index

Preface

For more than twenty years I have been following the trails of North America's mammals, an occupation that began as a hobby and turned into a commitment as the years passed. Today, in writing this book, I look back on a continent that has changed drastically in the comparatively short time since I first trod a wild path in the forest. Our cities have grown larger, our search for raw materials has pushed ever deeper into the hinterlands, driving many mammals to the brink of extinction by destroying their habitat and invading with huge machines the mountains, plains and forests that were once secure in their isolation.

Soon it may be too late for the average North American to see at first hand the marvels of our many animals as these pursue their lives in a magnificent wild world. Thus it is fitting, at this time, to write about my own experiences in the North American wilderness so that people everywhere may share, at least in part, its wonders.

Wildlife in North America: Mammals does not presume to be a complete guide to all the many species that inhabit this continent. Instead, I have attempted to capture the spirit of those wild things with which I have come into contact through the years and to pay tribute to them and to the wilderness that has for so long sustained them.

R. D. Lawrence
Gibson Lake, Ontario
June 1974

Babes in the Woods

It is a little larger than a honey bee, a minute pink blob whose eyes and ears are still undeveloped, whose legs are tiny pegs fitted with miniature claws. As it crawls blindly through the forest of hair, its stomach, heart and intestines are visible through the transparent covering of its body. This embryo, ejected from its mother's womb only thirteen days after it was conceived, should, one would think, perish within minutes of its premature birth. Yet slowly it climbs, its tiny stump legs barely moving, its wet, pink body glistening in the half-light of the tree den.

It is the mother opossum's first born, and if it survives the journey up her abdomen to the small entrance of her pouch it stands a chance to live. Within the pouch are warmth, safety, and thirteen pin-sized nipples offering nourishment.

Before long, sixteen more embryos are pushing instinctively through the jungle of their mother's hair, struggling to reach the pouch opening. At least four of these must die, for as each successful infant reaches a nipple and grasps it in his mouth, the nipple swells and causes a suction that makes it almost impossible to dislodge him. The latecomers will starve to death.

The first-born misses his footing. He tumbles down and lies wriggling on the debris-laden floor of the den. Soon he will be dead, completely ignored by the dozing mother.

Another embryo misses the mark and continues climbing past the small opening. He, too, will soon be dead, for he will receive no help from his mother.

The third baby finds the opening and locates a nipple. Safe.

Opossum family. The young are about ninety days old.

The fourth succeeds also, but the fifth, just as it reaches the opening, slips and falls. The sixth young 'possum dives through the hole and finds a nipple. Ten more find sanctuary in the pouch and affix themselves to the remaining nipples.

The mother moves slightly and the remaining three embryos are dislodged from their precarious holds. Did the opossum move deliberately? Did she know that all her nipples were now occupied? The questions do not matter. She has given birth, the proper number of infants are safe in her pouch; the others are expendable. It is nature's way and not to be questioned.

The thirteen babies that managed to crawl to safety will remain securely fastened to the mother's teats, sucking and dozing, for the next three weeks, never letting go.

Four weeks have passed and the thirteen small opossums are starting to move about. Tonight one of them tries to put his head out of the pouch opening while his mother is foraging for food, but she is able to flex a special muscle and close the opening against her young one's attempt.

An hour later she has eaten her fill and she seeks rest. Climbing higher up the pond apple tree to where three branches make a convenient fork, she drapes her body among them and anchors herself with her prehensile tail, wrapping it around one of the branches. She dozes.

Below her the sluggish water of the Florida everglades is dark and still. On the other side of the small hammock upon which the tree grows, a large alligator is preparing to slip into the water.

The daring young opossum again reaches the edge of the pouch and this time, because the mother is sleeping, he manages to poke his small head out of the opening. He wriggles a little more and now half his body is out, too.

Below, the alligator lies still, like some partly submerged log. The saurian has detected the movement in the pond apple tree. He likes opossum meat, and he remembers that at other times he has been rewarded by a careless young opossum that has tumbled out of its mother's pouch. He waits.

The young opossum is out of the pouch. He totters on his mother's belly and instinctively seeks to curl his tail around some object, to steady himself; but there is nothing. He slips, almost recovers, then falls. The splash made by his small body hitting the water is hardly audible, but the alligator is immediately on the move, sliding silently through the water. He opens his great jaws, closes them, and the baby is gone. The alligator moves away, submerges all but his knobby eyes and his nostrils and remains still, hopefully watching the tree.

Nine weeks later the mother 'possum is carrying her seven remaining young on her back, where they hang onto her coarse fur with hands and feet. Two more babies have fallen from the pouch and have been left to die in the jungle growth of the hammock floor. Three have died of starvation, for the mother did not have enough milk to keep all the babies alive and they were weakly and could not suck as vigorously as the others; when each one died the female 'possum reached into her pouch, picked it out, and discarded it.

Now the young are about the size of small rabbits and they will soon leave the mother to fend for themselves. They ride along with the mother until she stops to eat, then they scramble down and join in the hunt for insects, berries, or anything edible that they can find; it really doesn't matter, so long as it is food! Ground beetles, stink bugs, worms, moles, mice, lizards, birds' eggs, snakes, grasshoppers, ants, grapes, mulberries, mushrooms, persimmons, or carrion left by other creatures—anything will do.

With so much food available for the taking, it seems a wonder that opossums do not overrun the earth. But nature, as usual, provides a check: apart from the heavy toll exerted by the birth journey and the early weeks in the pouch, practically every predator large enough to kill one seeks the meat of North America's only marsupial.

Cougars, coyotes, foxes, bobcats, owls, hawks, alligators, ocelots, wolves, dogs, prey on the slow-moving 'possum—and, of course, man, for its meat tastes something like pork. The animal's only defense when cornered is to play dead, "to play 'possum", rolling over with its tongue hanging out, in a trance-like condition. Still, it is a tough animal and appears able to survive a variety of injuries that would kill almost any other creature.

Its normal range is from central New England to Florida and westward to the Great Plains, but it appears to be extending northward as far as southern Ontario and it is now well established from the Mexican border north to southern British Columbia, where it was introduced early in the twentieth century.

The adult opossum is about the size of a domestic cat, with a long sharp muzzle, short legs, and a long, naked tail that is covered in fine scales. Though its sparse, coarse hair may be a dark grey in the south, its color becomes lighter in the northern part of its range. In fact, the name "opossum" is an Algonquian Indian word meaning simply "white animal".

The Tunnelers

In autumn the forest floor is carpeted with wild bursts of color, the chill northern winds joust constantly with the tree-tops, the shrilling of wild geese echoes forlornly in the gray sky. The scene is at once lonely, beautiful, sad. The mind of a man turns back to the lost times of youth and remembers other days now gone forever. But for the animals of the forest, nostalgia has no meaning. For them only the demands of hunger and the spur of fear motivate action. The hunted seek not-yet-frozen bits of vegetation, while their ears and their eyes and their noses do sentry duty, forever wary of danger. The hunters stalk quietly, nostrils twitching for the scent of warm flesh, ears pricked up in quest of sound, eyes scanning the face of the bushland, alert for quick, furtive movement.

A large granite boulder squats immobile; its south face, sheared to plumb-line vertical, is covered in lichen, and on its crown stand withered ferns, like the gray hairs of age. South of this monolith is a dead pine tree, its girth defying the spread of a man's arms. The tree rests, its crown reduced to a tangle of rotten stems, its bark cracked and peeling.

From a tunnel in the piny punk a blue-gray head thrusts out into the air. It is small, with pointed snout, the jet-black eyes like minute baked currants in a bun. The pin-head nose quivers, the thread-like whiskers stick out, fine, living wires that shine silver in the last light of day. This is the shrew, and it is hungry again.

For a fraction of time it hovers at the gateway to its den, then its blunt, fine-furred body slips quickly into view and it drops onto the colorful autumn leaves.

A short-tailed shrew feeding on a meadow vole which it has just killed.

This small predator is insatiable in its quest for meat, being capable of eating the equivalent of its own weight every twenty-four hours. It is fast, fierce, bloodthirsty, and poisonous; a killer whose greatest enemy is its own hunger, for it moves so often and so quickly that it burns up energy like a miniature dynamo and must eat constantly if it is not to die wasted and weak. Even when it does sate itself, death is but a short pace away, for no animal this small and this voracious can survive for long the strain that constant hunting must put upon its body.

Now the rustle of dried leaves tells of the shrew's progress; occasionally a glimpse can be had of the gray body as it sets a course for a nearby beaver pond. This is a hunting route often followed by the shrew during its short life. The little killer knows that if prey is not encountered on the way to the water, some victim will almost certainly be found by the pond's edge, perhaps a frog, or a worm or two, or a salamander.

The mole-like hunter moves quickly, yet its senses are ever on the alert. Suddenly it stops. Ahead is a frog, hopping casually towards the water.

The shrew strikes, darting forward swiftly and attacking the frog before the amphibian knows what is happening. In an instant the shrew's sharp, orangy incisor teeth pierce the frog's brain, the poison mixed with the little killer's saliva entering uselessly into the wound, for the frog is already dead.

The frog is as big as the shrew, but the hunter easily drags the flaccid corpse to the shelter of a pile of leaves and there it settles to its meal. The little jaws move swiftly, tearing, pulling, chewing; in five minutes the shrew has eaten the head and shoulders and front legs of its victim; ten minutes later the killer is sated and all that remains of the frog is one back leg and part of the other. The shrew turns for home and sleep, its small belly distended.

Shrews eat anything. They are mainly carnivorous, but if nothing else is available they will eat vegetable matter. Carrion is prized and any young bird that accidentally falls from the nest is avidly devoured.

Once, many years ago, folklore said that the short-tailed shrew carried poison in its bite and people avoided the tiny hunter. Then came the age of enlightenment; science discounted the legend and the shrew's poison was forgotten.

But then some scientists became curious, and tests were made. These showed that the little short-tailed shrew has enough poison in its salivary glands to kill some 200 mice if both glands are dried, ground, and used as a mouse poison. And what is more, all the kinds of shrews that inhabit North America carry poison in their spittle, though that of the short-tailed shrew is the most potent, being likened to the venom of the cobra in diluted form.

17

When a short-tailed shrew bites, its poison flows into the wound, slows the heart of its victim and quickly reduces its breathing. The prey goes into a coma and the shrew quickly goes to work with its sharp teeth. Of course, the poison often is not needed, for the shrew dines royally on insects, worms and salamanders which it can master with ease; but in single combat with a mouse, which frequently outweighs its attacker, the poison swings the odds in favor of the hunter.

Because the shrew is always on the move, constantly prodded by his great hunger, his metabolism is so speeded up that he is doddering by the time he is one year old—if he lives that long, for he has enemies. Fox and hawk, weasel, mink and bobcat, lynx, coyote, owl, and even the timber wolf eat shrews. But some hunters are not overly fond of shrews, and will eat them only when they are really hungry, for the little killers have a pair of glands, one on each side of their body, at the flanks, that contain very strong musk.

This small hunter is not a sociable type. In fact, he is distinctly anti-social, the only other creature that can get along with him being his mate, and then only for relatively short periods of time, usually during the mating season and until the young shrews are born. Then the male goes off on his own, leaving the female to raise her litter of from three to ten pink, wrinkled mites, hardly larger than bees. As a rule the mother has six or seven babies; if one were to place all of these on a scale and balance them against two thin dimes, the coins would probably outweigh the brood!

Now the mother must hunt constantly to allow her body to provide the milk that her hungry little babies require during their first weeks of life.

A week or so after they are born their fur begins to grow, yet they are blind and toothless, and their ears are closed. But in another week their teeth begin to poke through the small gums and the ears open to their first sounds. Some ten days after this the eyes open. Now the female bundles her babies out of the nest. She is preparing to mate again, for she will have three or four litters in one year.

The mother may now move to a new den. Usually any number of these are available to her; she does not appear to be fussy. A cavity under a rock, an old mouse nest, a burrow in the ground, the inside of a rotten log, all these offer shelter to the shrew; inside her chosen shelter she will build a nest, a ball with an outside diameter of some six or seven inches containing a chamber about three inches across, the whole being built of dead leaves and grasses skillfully woven together.

All shrews look much alike. They are small with pointed muzzles, and ears so tiny that they are often completely hidden. Their general shape is sleek, almost torpedo-like, except when they have gorged themselves; then their full belly almost drags on the ground and gives them a distinctly round look. Shrew fur comes in various shades, from brown to gray-blue; the hair is short and silky and generally lies smooth.

Shrews are among the smallest of mammals. The long-tailed shrew is the largest North American species, measuring between three and six inches from nose to tail and weighing between one-third of an ounce and one ounce. The pygmy shrew is not only the smallest of the shrews; it is the smallest mammal in the world.

Perhaps one of the most interesting members of this family is the water shrew, a little creature about four inches long that swims and dives with ease and can actually walk on top of the water, its tiny feet being equipped with minute, silky hairs that trap air.

Although shrews are plentiful, few people recognize them for what they are, more often believing that they have seen a mouse or a mole on those occasions when a darting shrew has crossed their path. In fact, shrews bear little resemblance to mice; the latter are slightly larger, usually lighter in color, and have well-developed ears and coarser fur. As for moles, these are larger, slower, and are rarely seen above ground.

It seems hardly credible that a creature that is almost blind and weighs little more than four ounces can drive grown men to distraction, but that's what the mole can do, and often does. This little digger is seldom seen, as he spends practically all his time underground, but the trail of devastation that he leaves behind after a night's work beneath a prized lawn is enough to break a gardener's heart.

Yet the mole does more good than harm, lawns excepted! It is a voracious little creature that eats about a third of its own weight in worms and grubs every twenty-four hours. To do this, it must keep on the go constantly, aided only by its large, spadelike paws and a nose so sensitve that it can locate cutworms or Japanese beetle larvae in the pitch dark of its tunnels.

Like a swimmer doing the breast stroke, the mole uses its strong feet with their huge claws to excavate two kinds of tunnels: a network of deep ones, as much as two feet underground, and the shallow furrows that are the bane of gardeners. One of the deep tunnels ends in the den, a round chamber where the mole sleeps and spends the winter; in prolonged periods of heat and drought, he stays below and forages in the cool, moist earth of his subterranean runways. The surface tunnels are his usual forage routes and he can dig them at a rate of seventy-five feet a night, seeking out juicy tidbits to satisfy his ever-present hunger.

Most moles prefer open country where the soil is light and easy to dig—that's why they like well-cared-for lawns—and where there is an abundance of prey, though two species, the hairy-tailed mole and the shrew mole, prefer woodlands.

Moles mate only once a year, usually in March but earlier in warmer areas, and five or six young ones are born six weeks later. The babies are born in the underground den, which may be lined with dry grass or dead leaves, or may not be lined at all, depending probably on the availability of nesting material and the length of the tunnel that leads to the chamber. Young moles grow quickly and by the time they are two months old they are almost as large as their mother and are already getting about on their own and digging up the local golf course.

Most kinds of moles live solitary lives except at mating time. As they seldom emerge above ground except to gather nesting material or to deposit mounds of earth excavated from their deep tunnels, moles are relatively safe from predators; at these times, however, almost blind and with very

Star-nosed mole

poor hearing (moles have no external ears), they are easy prey for the meat eaters. If they avoid accidents, man's poison, or parasites that invade their bodies, they become senile at three years of age.

Mole fur is unique in that it is very short and velvety and will lie flat when stroked in any direction, thus offering little resistance as the animal tunnels through the soil. It is generally black or very dark gray.

In North America the common or eastern mole is the most widely distributed variety, ranging from Massachusetts westward to Minnesota and Nebraska and from Florida to Texas. It varies in length from five to eight inches and has a naked tail. Although its name is *Scalapus aquaticus* and its feet are partially webbed, it does not swim.

Another fairly common eastern species is the star-nosed mole, which has a strange, fleshy, starlike growth on the end of its nose. It lives from Labrador across Canada to Manitoba and south to Georgia and Illinois. This odd-looking creature is quite at home in the water, using its forepaws to swim in the same way as it tunnels through the ground. In the winter it sometimes runs over the surface of the hard-crusted snow. It is more sociable than most moles, often living in small colonies in marshes and damp fields.

Not too much is known about the hairy-tailed mole, which is rather scarcely distributed from New Brunswick and southern Ontario down through the mountains to North Carolina. It is a little smaller than the eastern mole and its short tail is covered with fur.

The western mole is the largest North American species, measuring seven to nine inches in length. It lives west of the Rockies from British Columbia to lower California.

West of the Sierra Nevada lives a strange little animal that is neither a mole nor a shrew, but somewhere in between. It is smaller than any of our North American moles, but not so tiny as a shrew. It has the shrew's long face, and front feet that are midway in size between the huge paws of the mole and the dainty little feet of the shrew. While the shrew mole, as it is aptly named, does some digging it frequently uses surface runways and will sometimes climb into small bushes in search of food.

Inventor of Radar

The little brown bat reels and swoops between the trees, mouth agape, white fangs gleaming even in the dark. From his throat pour ultrasonic cries, thirty of them every second, that bounce from leaves and branches. The bat swerves this way and that, skillfully avoiding the obstacles as his own voice, rebounding, warns him of their presence. He is cruising, hunting for the night-flying insects that are his sustenance.

Suddenly there is a change in the returning impulses. A small moth is flying some 200 feet ahead. Size of target, location, direction of flight and speed, all are picked up by the bat's short, pointed ears and translated by his brain into meaningful information.

The high-pitched cries accelerate. The bat flies rapidly in the moth's direction, but the moth has already detected the vibrations of its pursuer. It intensifies its zigzag flight, darting crazily up and down, in this direction and that. Guided by his own echo, the little brown bat pursues his prey, following every erratic move and dodging tactic.

The moth is doomed. Squeaking at a frenzied rate, the bat moves in for the kill. In another fraction of a moment the bat will intercept his moving target, using the membrane that surrounds his legs and tail as a scoop in which to capture the insect.

It is done. The bat's cries subside as he flies to a branch, hooks onto it with his feet, and hangs head down to consume his victim. Had this been a gnat or a mosquito or some other tiny insect, he would have eaten it on the wing, but this is a large meal and he rests while he devours it.

When the moth is gone the furry flier launches himself again into the black, moonless night in search of further morsels, for he must eat half his own weight in insects before morning. Clouds of gnats dance over the pond. Twisting and turning, darting with lightning speed, the bat captures 200 of them in the space of fifteen minutes, transferring them from wing to mouth faster than the eye can see. Frequently he dips to the surface of the pond to drink, for he must replace the moisture that is lost through the skin of his huge wings.

The hunting is good this night, there are many insects in the warm, humid air, and long before the first glimmer of dawn the bat, no longer hungry, flutters back to its perch in the barn to hang head down, like a limp brown leaf, to sleep away the day.

Bats are the only mammals that can fly. There are flying squirrels, true, but they merely glide, by spreading their legs and extending the fold of furry skin that runs between them, to form a kind of parachute. Only bats can propel themselves through the air, with wings that are constructed like a bird's though lacking flesh and feathers. The fingers of the bat, grown to monstrous length, are connected by a thin, elastic skin, forming true wings with which it can achieve perfectly controlled flight.

Bats are of very ancient lineage. Their fossil remains tell us that in the Eocene epoch, some 25 million years ago, when horses were still tiny creatures with four toes on each foot, bats existed in very much the same form as today. While most of their contemporaries had to change drastically in their structure and habits to meet changing conditions, or die, bats were so well designed and equipped that they could survive with very little basic alteration. But in these eons of time they have adapted when it was necessary to do so, and as a result there are today many hundreds of different species of bat, each perfectly suited to a certain way of life in some particular part of the world.

Little brown bat

All these many and various forms are grouped into numerous families, some of which live on fruit and a very few on animal blood. The great majority, however, live exclusively on insects and so are extremely beneficial to man. Three families are represented in North America. None of them north of the Mexican border drink blood, unless you count the body fluids of the six-legged creatures they consume.

Most bats are sociable creatures, though a few kinds prefer more solitary lives. Perhaps the most gregarious of all are the guano bats, which are abundant throughout the southern half of the United States. They inhabit caves, forming enormous colonies that sometimes number in the millions. The largest and most famous of these colonies is found in the Carlsbad Caverns, in New Mexico. Here live an estimated 8 million bats, and when they emerge at dusk to feed it is a spectacular sight. For twenty minutes they stream from the mouth of the cave like a great black river, spreading until the sky is filled with bats.

When you think of 8 million bats living in one cave, albeit a huge one that extends back into the rock a quarter of a mile and is 100 feet wide in places, you can imagine how this species got its name. Droppings accumulate on the floor of the cave at the rate of an inch per year, and the built-up deposit when this cavern was discovered was so thick that for fifteen years about 120 tons of this valuable fertilizer were extracted annually, and sold for prices between twenty and eighty dollars a ton.

The guano bats are very strong fliers and in the autumn they migrate, some as far as central Mexico, a distance of about 1000 miles. They belong to the family of free-tailed bats, so called because the tail projects beyond the wing membrane instead of being completely enclosed as in most other bats. There are several species in the United States.

Less common are the leaf-nosed bats, a few species of which occur in the southwestern States. They are of medium size and have a strange, fleshy, leaf-like growth on their nose. The most numerous is Waterhouse's leaf-nosed bat, which lives in caves in the desert regions of southern California, southern Nevada and Arizona; it is light grayish-brown and has large, rounded ears.

By far the largest number of North American bats belong to the family *Vespertilionidae*, which name derives from the Latin word *vespertilio*, meaning simply "bat". There are over twenty-five species of this family in the United States and Canada.

An extremely common member of this family is the little brown bat, which lives throughout North America from Alaska to Labrador and south to the southern United States. It lives in small to medium-sized colonies in almost every type of habitat from the forest wilderness to the heart of a big city, roosting in hollow trees, attics, barns, rock crevices and caves—yes, even in belfries!

Little brown bats gather in larger concentrations in winter to hibernate, as do many other bat species. At this time their body temperature drops to only slightly above that of the surrounding air, and they breathe as few as ten times in each hour. Even during their daytime roosts their blood cools somewhat, conserving energy in the tiny bodies which during their nightly forays have a temperature of 104 degrees Fahrenheit and draw breath about 200 times a minute.

Most bats mate in the autumn, just before they go into hibernation, but embryonic growth is suspended during their winter sleep, commencing as soon as they awaken in spring. From that time gestation takes an average of ten to fourteen weeks, depending on the species. There is usually only one baby, though twins and triplets are not uncommon in some kinds of bats.

At birth time, during May, June or July, the mother bat hangs upside down with all four limbs, using her thumbs, which are hooked projections on the front edge of her wings, as well as her feet. In this position she is able to spread her wings to form a sort of net into which the baby falls. She then licks it, attaches it to her fur, and nips off the navel cord.

For a few weeks the baby clings constantly to her underside, then it begins to make short flights around the roosting area, tutored by the mother. By this time it is growing heavy, and she may leave it hanging from the roost when she goes out to feed. Soon it begins to accompany her on hunting trips, and by four months it is fully grown and independent, though it will not be completely mature until it is about two years old.

If the young bat does not succumb to disease, or to some hawk or owl, it will probably live until it is five or ten years old, though some have been known to live as long as twenty. Should any damage occur to its ears, however, or even to one of them, it will very soon die, for without the full use of these sensitive receiving units the bat's marvellous radar system will break down. Then, if the bat is not destroyed by flying into some obstacle, it will quickly starve, as it will no longer be able to locate and capture its prey.

The Toothless One

The first armadillo that I ever saw outside a zoo was dead. It had been hit by an automobile and tossed to the edge of the road that links San Antonio to Laredo, in Texas, a piece of highway that cuts through semidesert country where vultures and tarantulas are common sights. I had, in fact, stopped the car to photograph a tree that was full of turkey vultures, their black bodies and bare red heads looking like some strange foliage decorating the otherwise stark branches.

As I stepped behind the car, I saw the body of the armadillo and I then realized that the vultures were awaiting the right moment to fly down and feed off its carcass, which, plump though it was (I judged it to weigh about sixteen pounds), would offer little enough to the fourteen vultures I counted in the tree. After I photographed the birds I stopped to examine the armadillo, sufficiently intrigued by the strange-looking creature to dare the rankness that 108 degrees of heat had produced in its body.

Texans in that area often refer to this armored survivor of an ancient order as "poverty pig", possibly because the armadillo looks a little like a queer, small hog, but more likely because its meat, properly dressed and cooked, is not unlike pork. Because there are many of them in the state and they are easy to hunt, anybody who is so disposed can enjoy roast armadillo.

I must confess that on looking close up at my first specimen I could see little resemblance to a hog. I was, I thought, looking instead at some miniature prehistoric monster, and that concept was much closer to the mark, for this armor-plated animal dates back to ancient times, when his ancestors grew to the size of a rhinoceros and inhabited the plains country of South America.

The specimen that I was examining measured twenty-nine inches in length and was six inches high at the shoulder. This, I later learned, was about average for an adult nine-banded armadillo.

Almost the only part of this armadillo that is not protected by armor is its long, sensitive nose! Its short legs are covered in hard scales and its tail is encased in a series of narrow, bony rings that restrict its movement only slightly. The creature's head is covered at the top and sides by a horny shield, while its body is almost encircled by two solid plates, one over the shoulders and front legs and one over the hips and back legs, the two plates united by nine bony bands which act as joints and allow considerable flexibility. But armor or not, the beast is almost toothless, being fitted only with a number of ineffectual molars that are not even covered with enamel!

At first I found this absence of teeth rather surprising. A creature so well endowed with bony material on the outside should, I thought, also have a full set of teeth inside its mouth. But later, after I had studied a number of them in various parts of Texas and Oklahoma, I realized that teeth were unnecessary to their existence. Nine-banded armadillos are peaceful creatures whose armor provides ample protection against the thorny underbrush of their habitat as well as against predators seeking their meat. They possess large, powerful claws, which they use for digging, and a long, sticky tongue that is able to collect fifty or sixty ants in one swipe. In this feature they resemble their relatives, the anteaters and tree sloths of South America, which are also virtually toothless.

The armadillo feeds almost exclusively on insects and similar creepy-crawly creatures, devouring great numbers of such delicacies as tarantulas, cockroaches, termites, beetles, scorpions, fire ants, centipedes, sugar-cane borers, grasshoppers, moths and any other "bug" they can stick their tongue to. Now and then they may eat some fruit or the odd mushroom, but they are not the quail-egg destroyers that some

Nine-banded armadillo

people accuse them of being; tests have shown that an armadillo really doesn't know quite what to do with an egg unless the shell has first been removed.

Armadillos are good swimmers once they have sucked a supply of air into their intestines. When they first enter the water they have trouble staying afloat and dog-paddle while they gulp down air, but once "inflated" they can swim easily for quite long distances. If the stream they are crossing is narrow, they simply walk across on the bottom, holding their breath and perhaps coming up once or twice for a quick gulp of air.

Typical habitat for these peculiar mammals consists of dense thickets, cactus patches, or clumps of chaparral or tall grass, where, because of the shade the vegetation provides, insects are plentiful.

They like to have several dens, perhaps as many as eight or ten, which are chambers at the end of earth tunnels that they dig for themselves. In each of these bedrooms, which are about sixteen inches in diameter, a nest of dry grasses is built, a sort of bundle into which the home-owner noses his or her way when it wants to sleep. Some of the numerous burrows are used only for emergency shelter, and in one of the dens the female gives birth to her young.

Mother armadillos invariably bear four young of the same sex, one more peculiarity of these strange mammals. This occurs because a single fertilized cell splits into four parts, resulting in identical quadruplets—and I mean identical! You just can't tell one baby armadillo from its litter mates. No one seems to know just why mother armadillos give birth to babies that are all of one sex, though it may be that this is nature's way of preventing brother and sister matings and thus keeping the breed strong.

The young are born in February, March or April. They come into the world with their eyes open and are fully developed, being able to walk about only a few hours after they are born, but their armor remains leather-soft until they reach adulthood.

The babies nurse for about two months, but several weeks before they are weaned they begin to forage with their mother and slowly develop their taste for insects, using their keen sense of smell to locate savory morsels and grubbing for them with their big claws. Often they dig furrows three or four inches deep in pursuit of their prey.

As a rule adult armadillos live alone in their dens, but they are nevertheless sociable animals, at times scurrying around in groups of twenty or thirty individuals.

The nine-banded armadillo is the only species found in the United States, ranging from Texas to southwestern Arkansas, eastern Oklahoma and Louisiana. It is also plentiful in Central and South America, where several other species of armadillo occur as well.

Eater of Trees

It is late February and the woods are basking in gentle sunlight. It is a day of rejoicing in the woods, one of those days that comes after a hard winter, a reminder that spring is near, that the sun, soon now, will drive away the cold that has gripped the land for five long months.

Today there is a special trill in the voices of the hardy birds that have stayed in the northland and dared the winter; the tiny, spritely chickadee varies its melodious call: *chickadee-dee-dee* . . . *chickadee-dee-dee* . . . *deee-dee-dee*. The blue jays scream joyously. Overhead a woodpecker dips and climbs on its way to feed on some rotten poplar or pine, to probe with its long beak for the grubs that hide under the wood.

It is a good day, gentle and quiet, and the forest yawns and stretches after its sleep. Punched into the melting snow, the tracks of an animal lead from under an old white pine stump, across a slight rise of ground, and end at the base of a young spruce. They are small marks, perhaps an inch and a half long by three-quarters of an inch wide; they look like miniature bear tracks and there is a directness of purpose in their line of travel. A stranger in the woods would wonder over their abrupt end. It looks almost as though the creature has started out from the young tree and walked backwards to disappear under the stump; but, no, this did not happen. The animal lives under the stump; it has emerged this morning, charmed by the sunshine, and has climbed into the tree. Soon pieces of the pine fall on the snow and a hopping snowshoe hare, glad of a change of diet, pauses to nibble at the tender needles, waiting to receive more of the unexpected tidbits.

Three hours have passed. The hare has gone, sated at last, and the snow under the tree is covered in green needles and small boughs and there are oblong, greenish droppings scattered around. The sun is at noon high, shining benignly on the woods and silhouetting a round, dark blob halfway up the tree, an immobile something wedged between two forked branches. At first glance it looks like one of last year's nests— perhaps the sticks and moss dwelling of a crow or the sturdy crib of a Cooper's hawk. There is something suggestive of life in that still shape. And life indeed there is, for the dark ball is a sleeping porcupine, replete after a feast of twigs and bark and dozing in the warm sun. Now and then one of its round, black eyes opens and focuses with disinterest on the goings-on around it. Stumpy back feet are curled upwards against its belly as the creature sits, its front legs almost folded across its breast, its rabbit-like head concealed by the arms and body. Indeed, until the creature moves, it is hard to tell which is its head and which is its tail, so compact is the ball.

The porcupine, a healthy young female, is unconcerned, as well she may be. There is nothing in this patch of forest that will harm her, and she knows it. She is slow, like all her kind, fat and lazy, an easygoing creature that minds her own business as she plods from her den to her feeding grounds. Gentle she is when undisturbed, but look out if a foolish one intrudes on her privacy!

There is an army at her call, a host of fine, needle-thin quills that sting like fire and cause death to most wilderness creatures. The quills grow on her head, on her back and sides and are especially thick and deadly on her short, broad tail. Aroused, she turns her back on her foe and raises all her mighty armament; just seconds before she looked to be just a fat, waddling ball of fur, but now, back hunched, blunt nose tucked down for protection between her front legs, and yellow quills ready, she looks as deadly as she is. The stubby, heavily-armed tail is raised slightly and quivers, ready for instant action as she swivels on her front legs, keeping her back always pointed at a circling enemy. A wolf, or a dog, may try to bite her. As the predator's open jaws close on their target, hundreds of barbed quills penetrate the mouth, the tongue

Porcupine

and the cheeks and while the hunter is trying to bite, chances
are that the fearsome tail will lash at the enemy's flank, leaving many of the barbs firmly anchored in the flesh. The
would-be killer howls in agony and begins biting at his hurt
while the porcupine waddles away to climb the nearest tree
or disappear into her den. But that is not the end for the attacker. Unable to rid himself of the fearsome darts, the creature eventually dies, that part of him in which the quills have
lodged slowly festering as the needles penetrate deeper and
deeper into the body. If the quills are sticking in his mouth
death comes quicker, because the predator cannot eat; but
slowly or quickly the porcupine's stings bring agonizing death
to those animals foolish enough to attack her.

The quills, which measure from about half an inch on the
sides and head, up to four and five inches on the back and
tail, are the color of fresh ivory, with a fine, black point. On

this point, so tiny they are almost invisible, are the barbs, set one behind the other. As soon as the barbs dig into flesh, the quills come loose from the porcupine's body. They are attached to the porcupine by a thin "stalk" at their base which is connected to a layer of muscle that lies just under the skin; when the porcupine contracts this muscle, the quills rise.

Usually the forest meat eaters avoid the porcupine. Only during times of great cold and famine will a wolf or a bobcat, a cougar or a lynx attack the cumbersome creature. Sometimes the porcupine loses, but rarely; almost always the killers themselves die. But there is one who preys successfully on the porcupine: the fisher, a large killer of the weasel family that is as swift as lightning and as savage as the wolverine. The fisher has learned the porcupine's weakness, the soft, unprotected belly; quicker than the eye can see, it shoots out a paw and turns the porcupine on its back. In a flash the killer rips open the belly and there is one porcupine less in the woods.

Once there were many fishers and many porcupines and only the Indians killed them so that their women could use the quills, colored with plant dyes, to decorate moccasins and buckskin leggings. There was an even balance in the forest. Fishers killed porcupines to live; Indians killed them for their quills and their flesh. Just enough were killed so that the forests thrived, for the porcupine, living in winter on an almost exclusive diet of tree bark and twigs, is a destroyer of timber.

Then came the greatest predator of all, the white man, and he quickly discovered the value of the fisher fur in the far markets of Europe. The white traders encouraged the Indians to kill fishers and in exchange gave them colored beads and other things. The Indians no longer killed as many porcupines for their quills because now they had the beads to use for decoration. So, the fisher gradually became scarce and the porcupine, safe from practically all other predators, thrived and soon the white man discovered that the bristling fellow with the slow movements was an enemy of the forest.

The balance of nature was disturbed. The porcupine, designed for a purpose, did not start out to be a killer of forests, but was made so through the ignorance of man. Only in the far north, where the fishers withdrew from civilization, does the natural balance remain. Elsewhere, white men with guns must shoot the sitting porcupines out of the trees they have ravaged, or they will multiply so greatly that the life of all in the forest will be at stake.

Fortunately the creatures mate in the autumn and gestation is long; it takes the baby porcupine 210 days to get ready to be born; and porcupine mothers rarely have more than one baby at a time.

Usually these woodland creatures are silent, but now and then they can be heard making strange noises; sometimes they squeak and these sounds are almost human. They moan also, but the sound does not express sadness or pain; it is just a way of saying something, usually to themselves, for porcupines are solitary fellows.

Only in the fall, during the mating season, which begins in October in the south and extends to December in the north, do the animals mingle, and then the males will bristle and grunt at each other like two angry old men; but they rarely attack, probably because each knows what it can expect from the other!

After the mating the porcupines go their respective ways. The female looks for a good winter home, usually under an old stump, or in a rock cave, or even in an old skunk burrow if there's nothing else handy, and the male picks out a piece of territory for himself. Each now eats and eats and eats, preparing its fat layers for the winter and exploring its home ground, and when snow comes they can be seen on sunny days in the trees, stripping bark with their long, yellow teeth, or picking at pine or spruce needles. They are settled in for the winter; from now on they will not go more than a few hundred feet in any direction from their burrow, not until spring, that is, when they will again start wandering, feeding on brush and small vegetation and leaving the trees alone. This is just as well, because though not very large (an adult will weigh between ten and fifteen pounds, and, now and then, as much as thirty) they can eat their way through a lot of green food and once they girdle a tree with their sharp teeth, it will die.

It is late May. The snow is gone. Tender young leaves rustle in the aspens and the forest is alive. It is evening and already a whip-poor-will is uttering its monotonous song again and again while swallows swoop and dive, picking up mosquitoes as they zoom gracefully between the trees.

Under the old pine stump new life is about to emerge. The mother porcupine is lying concealed in the darkness of her burrow, clenching her stomach muscles as her baby pushes to reach life. Already the mother has been long giving birth, but the moment is almost here now. There is no warm nest awaiting the youngster, for this is not the way of porcupines; anything will do for the new baby, a burrow like this one, or a rock overhang, or the bare ground under some downed tree.

It is done now. Slowly the mother turns in her den and smells for her baby; her shoebutton eyes are useless in this darkness, but her keen nose scents the new life she has made. The baby is still encased in its birth membrane, and the mother must bite through the sac and clear it away so that her little one may breathe. She does this, and the half-pound youngster squirms free of the jelly-like covering. The little one is about twelve inches long from the start of his stubby tail to the tip of his black, round nose. His black eyes are already open and his front teeth, those yellow-orange weapons which he will use later to strip bark from the trees, are already formed. So are his quills. They are soft yet, and almost smooth, but in another hour or so, when he is dry, they will be hard and sharp and he will be able to use them to defend himself.

The Tree Dwellers

Scudding across the face of a full moon the clouds cast shifting patterns of shadow on the crusted snow. It was mid-March, and though the night was crisp with frost some of the forest's creatures were out looking for mates. Male skunks chittered spitefully at one another somewhere under a pine; a young he-raccoon made small, crunching sounds as he tramped along, driven by the urge to breed.

In the middle of a patch of mixed woodland nestled a small cabin; it was a simple structure, a frame building twelve feet wide by eighteen feet long, the unpainted pine siding glowing a rich cream in the moonlight, the red shingles of its roof looking brown under the diffused beams. The cabin's only door faced west and one small window looked in the same direction, past a young white pine.

The pine stood eight feet from the cabin; hanging from one of its horizontal lower branches was a wire-netting cone which had been filled with beef fat, an offering of nourishment for many of the small creatures that lived within sight of the building. In the daytime that cone and others nearby attracted a variety of species: black-capped chickadees, the fluffy, perky gymnasts of the bird world, stopped often to take a beakful of food; bright, raucous blue jays leaned down from the branches and pecked at the yellowish substance; nuthatches, short stubby birds that walk as easily upside down as they do upright, chanted their nasal calls between morsels of suet. Now and then a hairy woodpecker came to eat, landing on the cone and bracing its body with its stiff, bristly tail.

Other creatures, too, visited the fat stations. Red squirrels, cheeky and chattering, cursed each other as they vied for position and big black squirrels, members of the gray squirrel clan, found the fat and ate of it.

They were busy in the daytime, those hanging lumps of grease, but at night it was different: the tree creatures and the birds were gone. Many beasts that shun daylight hunt on the ground, and so most of the fat stations hung listless, their dead cells crystalizing under the attack of the frost and casting minute green and blue flashes each time the air gave movement to the tree boughs.

In the pine beside the cabin stealthy life was busy at the fat. An elfish face, with big, protruding eyes that shone ruby red in the moonlight, hovered above the cone; a small, brown body that was dressed in silky fur and ended in a three-inch bushy tail was outlined behind the face. The little beast had fine black whiskers, short ears and tiny, hand-like paws that were gripping the wire cone; a loose mantle of skin ran along both of its flanks, from front legs to back legs. Now this skin was neatly folded in sculpted pleats that were heaviest at the shoulders. The creature was hardly bigger than a two-week-old kitten.

It spent ten minutes nibbling at the fat, then it withdrew to a higher branch where it sat washing its dainty face; afterwards it scuttled higher up the tree, until it was about forty feet from the ground, sitting bunched on the topmost branch. It hung poised a moment, then it launched itself away from the tree with its back legs. As soon as it was clear of the pine's branches it spread all its limbs wide and the skin on its sides unfolded, meeting the pressure of air and billowing like a small sail, sustaining the light body. For perhaps four seconds the shadowy figure glided through space, describing a descending arc which carried it towards the branches of a larger pine fifty feet away. When it was immediately above the middle branches of this tree, the creature lowered its back legs and the spread skin became an air brake; it landed lightly, gripping one of the branches with its hind feet. Scurrying along, it reached the rough trunk and disappeared inside a hole in the tree. The flying squirrel had filled its small stomach tonight; now it would sleep.

39

The orange glow from an early sun bathed the cabin and turned its raw siding a warm yellow. A red squirrel was busy at the cone of fat in the pine tree. He was a handsome male, his back and tail a deep chestnut red, his sides paler, turning to white on his belly and there were twin etchings of white surrounding his dark, protuberant eyes; almond-shaped and clear, these splashes gave the squirrel a wide-eyed look.

Busy gnawing at the fat, the young buck stopped suddenly and looked about him, his rounded ears pricked forward, his nervous little body ready to explode into flashing action if danger was near. In another moment anger tinged his peaked face and he chittered furiously, at the same time stamping his back feet against the tree branch in a fast rhythm of annoyance. His mouth was open, his tawny throat quivering as he voiced a warning to another of his kind who was even then nearing the trunk of the tree, hopping quickly along the ground, his bushy tail, like a miniature plume, sticking up in the air. The intruder paused at the foot of the pine, looking up, as though debating whether or not to risk a fight with the early feeder.

The buck in the tree was the original "homesteader" in the cabin area and had staked his claim on the supplies of seed and fat which the cabin owners put out every Saturday morning. This is the way of red squirrels. They are solitary little fellows and, apart from a brief time during March when the mating urge is strong, they live alone, each keeping to his own territory and ready to fight to the death any of his kind that dares to invade the chosen acre or so of bushland in which he lives. Usually squirrels respect each other's territory, now and then passing the time of day with their neighbors from a distance, but the area around the cabin was different; man had come here and he had provided much food for the forest dwellers and all the other squirrels in the area came to help themselves. At first the original "owner" fought and scolded and did his best to chase the intruders away, but as the days passed eight or ten of his neighbors came at one time and the outraged landowner suddenly discovered that while he was busy chasing one squirrel, the others were eating. About the only one who went hungry in the area around

Red squirrel

the cabin was the rightful master of the domain, who was too busy chasing poachers to stop and eat of the fat and the seeds that were there.

At last the red buck gave up. He staked the best claim, the one where the greatest amount of seed was placed, and provided that his neighbors left him alone while he was eating—and this was often—he made no attempt to chase them; he did not like the company, but he had little choice in the matter and was forced to compromise, now and then, after he had packed his round belly with food, squatting sleepily on a big pine near his food supply and cursing those who came to eat.

The squirrel on the ground started up the tree, and this was the final outrage. The red buck redoubled his stamping and his cursing, then down he came, a blur of movement so fast it was almost impossible to follow. The two animals ran round and round the pine, both chittering now, the intruder only just keeping out of reach of the furious teeth that flashed inches from his rump; then the poacher slipped slightly, recovered and ran on, but the red buck had gained and in another moment his long, chisel-sharp teeth flashed and the escaping squirrel felt the sting of the bite on his back. With a final, protesting squeal of rage and frustration, the interloper ran down the tree and streaked across the ground to disappear under a pile of brush.

The red squirrel went back to his fat and finished his meal. Afterwards he climbed through the tree and passed into the next pine, his favorite resting place; curled up close to the trunk, safe from the death dive of the hawk that lived nearby, he dozed.

At birth red squirrels are pink and tiny and naked; they weigh little more than an ounce apiece as they lie inside their nest. Most of them are born during late April or early May, about thirty-six days after the mating. The nursery may be an old woodpecker hole in pine or oak or cottonwood, or a carefully built nest of sticks and moss high up in a pine or spruce. Usually five or six babies are born to the mother squirrel and though they will grow into agile, handsome little animals, at the moment of birth they are ugly mites indeed; including the scraggly tails they are barely four inches long, their heads seem too big for their bodies and their noses are blunt. Red and wrinkled, and with big eyelids hiding bulbous eyes, only a devoted mother can love them when they first enter the world and it is not until nine or ten days later that they begin to look like squirrels.

At seven weeks they start exploring the outside, hesitant and timid at first, gradually gaining strength. They often fall to the hard ground below, but, such is their agility, they always seem to manage to twist in mid-air and land on their feet, apparently unhurt by their experience, yet terrified and calling for mother to come and get them.

By late summer the youngsters leave home and each finds and claims an acre or so of woodland which is jealously guarded. These squirrels always seem to be aware of all that is happening around them; if an intruder enters their domain, the tiny watchdogs are quick to report the fact to all the creatures of the woods. Sitting or standing on some branch high in a tree, they shrill and chatter incessantly until the intruder has gone. Their alarm is often taken up by the jays and the crows and at such times the forest becomes a place of many noises.

Red squirrels gather their food supplies all year around; in spring and summer they eat most of what they pick off the trees, but in the autumn they start storing their winter supplies, caching seeds and berries and bits of mushroom under a pile of brush, inside a hollow log, under a rock or even in the grass; some of these hoards may contain several bushels of nuts and seeds, others may be just small hiding places capable of concealing only one or two hazelnuts or a dozen or so hemlock or pine seeds.

Winter does not seem to hold any fears for the red squirrels. During severe storms they hole up in their dens, but as soon as the wind drops and the snow stops falling, out they pop, scurrying through hemlock or pine in search of food, for they seem to prefer to save their stored supplies "for a rainy day" if they can. When the snow becomes deep enough they tunnel under it, crossing open spaces this way, safe from hunting birds or other meat eaters, and usually these tunnels lead to one or more of their food piles.

The red squirrel lives in trees, travels through them and collects most of his food from them, but he also spends a lot of time on the ground. When feeding in a hemlock he will strip the small cones right from the branches and fill his cheeks with the seeds, but the large pine cones are first cut off from their boughs and tossed to the ground. When a number of these are down, the squirrel follows them and carries one to the vantage of a log or a rock, where he separates the seeds from their woody overcoats.

The forests are full of these inquisitive and alert creatures, though they fluctuate in mysterious cycles; at times the woods are teeming with them, at other times it is hard to find more than one or two in a ten-acre patch.

Of course they have enemies. Hawks, owls, weasels, mink, bobcat and lynx are always seeking a meal of squirrel flesh, but the most persistent, dangerous predators of the red squirrel are the fisher and the pine marten; these big, weasel-like killers can travel through the trees faster than the squirrels and unless the little fellows can find a hole too small for the hunters to crawl through, they die after a furious tree-top chase.

Red squirrels, like all of their other relatives, eat anything. Their chief foods are the seeds of evergreens, and hazelnuts, but fruit in season, tree bark, carrion and even small birds and mammals as well as some insects are devoured by them. In the presence of man they quickly learn to take his handouts and soon lose all fear if they are not molested.

When night comes again to the woods and the red squirrels are asleep in their nests, their flying cousins take over; these gentle animals are perhaps the most interesting of the squirrel clan. They are friendly, yet extremely shy and seldom go about during daylight hours. Their diet is similar to that of the red squirrel, but while their relative is jealous of his supplies and prefers his own company, the flying squirrel likes to have others of his kind near him.

As a rule two or three young ones are born in a tree den, though some females have given birth to as many as seven; the little ones weigh scarcely one ounce and they are blind and deaf when they come into the world. The skin which allows them to glide is already formed, folded and transparent against the dark pink, hairless body. At this time the little ones receive special care and devotion from their mother; she nurses them constantly, taking only a few moments at a time to go out and eat, and she is fearless when it comes to protecting her young. If a man takes one of her brood she will run out of her nest and climb up the intruder's clothing to snatch the baby from his very hands and return with it to her tree; expertly she rolls the baby into a tight ball and grasps it by the skin of its belly, and away with it she goes.

There are great numbers of flying squirrels in the forests of North America, but not many people see them. Occasionally a late-feeding squirrel is noticed as it glides back to its nest-

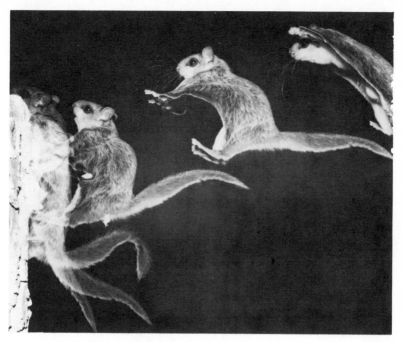

Flying squirrel, photographed using stroboscope

ing tree, but unless man is out at night in the forest he may live in an area that sustains many of these little creatures and never know they are his neighbors.

Standing quietly in a pine forest at night one can often hear these small acrobats as they talk to each other; their voices are soft, their calls a high-pitched sound rather like the chirping of a cricket. Follow the sound and sooner or later one finds a squirrel, usually busy feeding, and if one shines a flashlight on him he does not run off; his big eyes shining ruby under the light, he continues eating, now and then blinking at the glare, and it is only when one approaches too close that he takes fright; then, in a flash, he is gone, leaving no trace but a gently-swaying bough.

The Sleepers

A thick layer of snow seals the brown earth. Rocks and small
shrubs are hidden and the forest is a shining contrast of ever-
green and white that is capped on this day by the pastel blue
of a sun-filled sky. It is cold, twenty degrees below zero, but
it is not unpleasant in the forest. Some of the hardy birds are
flitting about in the trees, the gray jays and the chickadees,
the blue jays and the woodpeckers, and their chatter is pleasant to listen to.

Under a young and naked poplar there is a hump in the
snow. The small tree's spindly shadow falls on this mound,
and were it possible for eyes to see through the frost crystals,
the shape and color of a large granite rock would be visible
under the white covering. When it split from its matrix the
chunk of granite took the form of a rough triangle; its apex
fell downwards and the weight of the inert body drove it into
the ground, so that it balanced there, leaving a space between
its upper points and the earth. Around the rock, under the
shelter of its overhangs, are three holes. Each is about nine
inches in diameter and each goes down into the ground at an
angle; in front of the holes are little mounds of earth, made
when the creature that excavated the holes dumped surplus
earth outside them. But all this is hidden now and there is
only a white bump marking the site.

Opposite the poplar, about ten feet away, grows a small
white pine. The little tree is rooted in rocky ground and it
has not done well; it is stunted, its lower arms are dry and
brittle and its crown is distorted; still it serves a purpose.
Now the branches are covered in snow and the white has

crept two feet up the trunk. Under the snow, near the trunk, there is another hole, a small tunnel that goes straight down for five inches and then slopes off and continues a more gradual descent.

The poplar and the pine and the rock are neighbors in the wilderness, and so are the occupants of the tunnels. Under the rock lives a brown, cautious woodchuck; down in the burrow under the pine lives a tiny, inquisitive chipmunk. Both are now asleep. While the cold frosts the world outside and while some of the creatures of the wilderness perish from hunger, the chipmunk and the woodchuck slumber soundly, impervious to the weather and the hunters, secure and snug in their dens.

Both of these creatures are true hibernators. The woodchuck beds down in a matting of dry grass and rolls up in a ball by tucking its head between its hind legs and clasping its front paws around its shoulders, and it sleeps. Its breathing slows almost at once and gradually becomes fainter as the woodchuck's body gets colder; the pulse is feeble and at last breathing almost stops altogether and only a trickle of oxygen reaches the slowly moving lungs. The body temperature can drop as low as forty-two degrees Fahrenheit.

Meanwhile, the pastel-shaded chipmunk is also sleeping in his smaller burrow a few feet away, but there is a difference in the two creatures; whereas the marmot will sleep soundly until spring comes, feeding off its stored fat, the chipmunk will wake up on mild days and feel the pangs of hunger. Then it is a simple matter for the tiny woodsman to enjoy breakfast in bed; in fact, his bed is also his pantry! During the late summer and early fall this quick, friendly fellow packs seeds and nuts into two capacious pouches in his cheeks and carries them to his bedroom, looking as though he has an acute attack of the mumps; by winter the food in his sleeping chamber almost touches the ceiling and then, when the cold is intense outside, the chipmunk climbs onto his bed-larder and curls up.

As the winter grows tired, the stores under the chipmunk shrink and by spring the little creature is sleeping almost on the hard earth. Now and then, when the weather has turned mild outside, he scrambles off his bed and pops up in the snow for a quick look at the forest world. He may spend minutes or an hour or two romping about, then down he goes, probably to have a quick supper before coiling himself up again.

The woodchuck and the chipmunk are both sound winter sleepers, but this habit ends the similarity between them. The woodchuck weighs between five and ten pounds and is a slow-moving, plump, rather stupid fellow; the chipmunk weighs about three ounces and is as fast as a streak of light, intelligent, friendly and definitely curious. The chipmunk is a pretty creature in his rusty coat set off by black and white stripes. Perhaps because of his speed, the chipmunk is daring where the woodchuck is timid. The little fellow will soon learn to come for tidbits put out by humans and in no time will make fast friends with man if he is not scared away by dogs or cats or small boys with sling-shots. But the waddling marmot will not respond in this way. It will take food if this is placed by its den, but only after the human has gone. It will come out of its hole to inspect an intruder, cautiously peeping over the mound of earth before one of its doorways, ducking back quickly and emerging again a few moments later if it thinks the coast is clear.

Under the snow and the rock and two feet below the earth the woodchuck is curled up in his winter chamber, an "apartment" about sixteen inches in diameter and nine inches high; the creature lies on a mattress of dry grass and leaves and he has built his bedroom higher than the middle section of his tunnel to protect himself against sudden thaws and flooding of his quarters. There is a short, steep tunnel connecting the sleeping room with the main underground passage, which runs almost forty feet from its entrance by the granite rock, past the bedroom and on, to emerge under a bush near a patch of blueberries. This sleepy, clumsy fellow never builds his home with a single tunnel; usually there are one or more

Groundhog, or woodchuck

forks and several side passages and rooms and one of these is usually a toilet, for the creature is clean and if he cannot go outside to deposit his dropping on the mound of earth by the entrance to his burrow, he reserves one room for this necessary function.

During winter, of course, he has no need of his toilet, for all such body functions cease with hibernation and don't begin again until the woodchuck opens his small black eyes during a warm day in later winter.

March is the time of waking for the woodchuck. The snow is still on the ground, but stronger sunshine is attacking it and the ends of last year's grasses, dry and frostbitten, begin poking through the crusting layer of white that has concealed them for five months; inside the dark bedroom the new warmth reaches the woodchuck's body and stirs life into his sluggish blood. The breathing begins to quicken and soon the animal moves, stretches, opens his eyes and decides it is time to go up and see the world again.

The tunnel entrance may still be crusted with snow when the woodchuck pokes a cautious head just over the rim of his burrow. First to the left, then to the middle and then to the right the careful beast looks, his rounded ears and twitching nose helping the keen eyes to detect signs of danger. Rarely does the woodchuck come straight out of his tunnel, however; usually he sits inside it, some six inches from the entrance, and he listens and sniffs for a full ten minutes before thrusting his head out. If all is well, he climbs up onto his mound and stands erect, front legs held loosely across his chest, and he takes another good look around before daring to waddle a short distance away and begin nibbling on twigs or dried grasses and shrubs; but for all his clumsy pace, if danger threatens suddenly the woodchuck can run surprisingly fast and is usually able to reach the safety of his den—but not always!

In March the woodchuck breaks one of the rules it lives by; normally it never wanders more than 100 yards from its home for feeding, but in spring, when the mating urge is strong, it ranges quite far in search of females. This is the season of fighting for the males; mild, fearful and slow they may be in ordinary times, but during the breeding season they are veritable demons when they meet a rival. Panting and growling furiously, they grind their cheek teeth and charge an opponent, chewing his ears or tail or body, and these battles may sometimes last as long as half an hour before one of the fighters admits defeat; the loser may leave the scene with half his tail missing and the winner may well have only one good ear left.

Male woodchucks sometimes seek one mate after another or they may mate with the first one they meet and settle down with her until the young are born; then they are ejected from the den and have nothing more to do with their family and they go and live the life of a hermit until next mating time.

The young woodchucks are born about four weeks after mating. Usually four little ones arrive, but from two to the exception of nine may be born. They are naked and pink, wrinkled and blind, and they weigh between one and one and a half ounces and are less than four inches long, including their ratty little tails. For the first four weeks of life they feed from their mother, but after that their eyes open and they begin to explore the outside world, stumbling about the den entrance and nibbling at green food. By midsummer the mother finds her den crowded with her fast-growing children and she drives them off to find homes of their own in the vicinity of her burrow, where she can keep an eye on them until they leave in the autumn to look for permanent homes.

The woodchucks are day feeders and solitary creatures. They like sunshine and love to lie near their dens sunbathing after they have been out to eat. Usually they come out early in the morning, eat, then return to their den entrance, where they sit for one to three hours, but when the sun begins to climb towards the noon position, down they go into their burrows, to sleep in the cool. Sometimes, when the moon is full and the night is warm, they emerge after dark to feed and then they are doubly cautious, for the meat eaters are always seeking to devour the roly-poly marmot.

Anything green is food for the woodchuck and around the cultivated field it is a menace; its bulging stomach can hold as much as one and a half pounds of greenstuff at a time and what it does not eat it often tramples down. If the woodchuck does any good at all for the farmer it may be in the one per cent of bugs and grasshoppers it eats, but this is little repayment for the damage that the creature can do to a budding field of corn or alfalfa!

If the marmot is clumsy and cautious, his little neighbor is just the opposite. He dashes about the forest at a great rate and stops often to inspect man or beast, intent on all that he meets during the course of his travels. In February, during warm spells, the chipmunk pops up out of his burrow and starts looking for a mate; it is far too early for the females to breed, but this does not stop the little chap, who often gets a good hiding from an aroused lady when he scrambles down into her bedchamber. Chirping pain and anger at the harsh treatment, the chipmunk escapes, but doesn't stop looking for

Chipmunk

a mate until after he has aroused passion in the breast of some pretty lady in his vicinity, and this usually happens in March.

While there is nothing daintier or more spritely than the adult chipmunk, there is hardly anything so small and wrinkled and puny as chipmunk babies. The little ones arrive thirty-two days after the mating and there are generally four or five of them. Red, hairless and almost transparent, they squeak faintly as they search for their mother's milk. When two weeks old, baby chipmunks have a short fuzz all over their bodies and they can stand up, but they are still deaf and will be for another week and their eyes will not open until they are four weeks old. At three months they are almost adult and they leave home and seek their living in the forest.

Though they live alone, they are not as solitary as the marmot and they are much more loquacious; the woodchuck will whistle in times of danger, but the chipmunk often chatters all day long, especially during the autumn. His call is a soft *cuck-cuck-cuck* repeated over and over and often the little fellow will repeat his "song" for half an hour without stopping.

The chipmunk gets up early; daybreak finds him out and looking for food, which consists mainly of fruit, nuts, seeds, and a variety of plants and mushrooms in season; he also likes meat and eats large numbers of insects, but if he is useful in this regard he can be quite destructive in another, for the pretty little fellow loves birds' eggs and young birds and will take them whenever he can. Of course, there are beasts in the wilderness, and birds, that love to eat chipmunks and so nature has provided a balance between her species.

Even though there are some bad sides to the chipmunk's nature, he is, nevertheless, a handsome, friendly chap and he and his neighbor, the woodchuck, are a colorful part of the wilderness. When the autumn comes to drive them underground there is always a little sadness in the event, for their absence from the forest signifies the death of another summer and the start of the time of hardship for many wild creatures.

Season of Plenty

Dawn was a misty canvas daubed with blue and green and the red of a big, round sun. Somewhere out on the lake, its sleek shape low on the water and concealed by the gently swirling mist, a loon shrieked its maniac laugh as the big, duck-like bird disported itself during its favorite time.

The surface water was placid, like a huge mirror reflecting sky and trees and stained by the sun's redness. A minnow, lured from the green depth by a speck of flotsam on the water, swam up, opened its small mouth and poked at the minute piece of bush waste it had mistaken for food; when it retreated, spitting out the inedible particle, it left behind a slowly widening ring on the surface. For perhaps two minutes the scene remained so: the sky and the sun and the mist and the loon. And then, silence.

On three sides of the lake, pine and poplar jostled for growing room almost to the water's edge; on the south side a granite escarpment dropped sheer and gray into the depth, its rough surface pockmarked here and there with small growing things, tenacious bits of life that had found footing in soil-filled cracks.

Close to the granite wall a small rock island arched out of the water. Its naked surface would have resembled a giant stone mushroom, but it was now covered by an untidy mound of sticks that were packed here and there with crusted mud from the lake bottom. The mound was some ten feet in circumference and had been built over a deep cleft on the island, and dry sticks, placed off-center on their support, extended down into the water.

Movement agitated the water near the peeled sticks and a shaggy face emerged. The beaver appeared to snort, ejecting a tiny spray of water from his nostrils as the valves within his nose opened to admit air into the extra-large lungs; on the surface the valves would stay open, but they would close automatically the moment the animal went under.

The beaver paddled slowly away from his lodge, surveying the lake with small eyes and gradually altering his straight course, sweeping along now in a semicircle, moving faster, the wake from his thick body spreading in a V behind the kicking, webbed back feet.

The swimming beaver increased his speed, kicking harder with his big feet and using his twelve-inch-long, flat, scaly tail to steer a course to the west side of the lake, where a compact group of poplars promised succulent feeding. As he swam, a shadow passed over his head. Immediately what sounded like the report of a rifle-shot shattered the early morning silence. It was the beaver's tail, which the animal slapped vigorously against the water, a warning to his kind that there was danger about. Even before the reverberating echoes faded to dull whispers up-lake, the beaver sounded, while the great, gliding shape of a golden eagle sailed overhead, retracting the talons it had begun lowering towards the water.

It is doubtful that the eagle would have seized the beaver, or having seized it, been able to pull it clear of the water, but the seventy-pound rodent was taking no chances that day; he stayed concealed and safe in the glassy deep of his domain for fifteen minutes, enabled to remain this long without fresh supplies of air by the big lungs and extra large liver, which store great amounts of oxygen.

When he broke surface again it was close to the poplar shore, and with hardly more than a hasty glance around, as though he had already forgotten the recent danger, he waddled out of the water, an ungainly black shape on land that dripped moisture from his shiny fur. This beaver was eight years old and the head of a clan of seven animals, one of which was his mate, the other five his offspring of two seasons, two of them one-year-olds, the others born that spring.

Beaver

He was about early that morning and had left his lodge
before the others had come fully awake, for he was hungry.
Now he was making for the canal the family had built last
year to allow them to reach the poplars in safety.

This channel was a short one, only some seventy feet long.
In another area, depending on the distance the beaver had to
travel to reach their food trees, it might have extended several hundred feet and reached as much as two feet in width by
as many in depth. On that summer morning the beaver landed twenty feet from his canal and walked to it, though, had
he wished to, he could have swum straight to its entrance under water and continued his trip submerged right up to the
nearest poplar.

The big rodent slipped into the canal and paddled lazily up
it; before he reached its end he climbed the steep bank and
stopped to shake himself before shuffling towards a tree he
had started cutting the night before. He paused before it, sur-
veyed it for a moment and decided he would not be both-

ered with it. It was a big tree, some two feet in circumference and already half cut, but the beaver was fussy today. He walked on and now paused beside a smaller tree, scarcely thicker than a man's fist. After inspection, he appeared satisfied and he reared on his hind legs, using his flat tail as a brace for his body.

He began work, seizing the tree at eye-level and cutting a notch in it with his lower teeth, the big buck teeth at the top holding on to the trunk. Soon the chips began to fly and the first notch was cut. Shifting his hold on the tree to a spot three inches lower the beaver cut a second notch, then he seized the green wood between these notches and wrenched a piece out of the trunk. He worked on, moving around the tree, gnawing at it until a V-shaped furrow encircled the tree. The tree began to lean towards the lake, slowly at first, then it gathered speed and plunged, crashing in a welter of green. The beaver quickly slipped into his canal and swam down it rapidly, entering the lake and remaining under the water for several minutes; when he appeared again, he stayed on the surface but made certain the falling tree had not attracted some enemy to the scene of his labors. When he was sure the coast was clear, he returned to the tree and settled down to his breakfast, peeling the cucumber-flavored bark from the white wood with his sharp teeth.

At this time of the year, the beaver and his family had little to worry about; now and then the patriarch would visit the dam, that curved like a crescent moon across the mouth of a creek. If the old beaver found a weak spot in the walls he would repair it, towing sticks and poking them into the wall, then diving for an armful of mud which he would carry against his chest while he waddled on his back legs, using his tail as additional support. If the break in the wall was large, the whole family would be turned out and they would work hard and fast until the hole was plugged.

Not all beaver build dams. Some live in dens excavated in the banks of rivers, the entrances to which are deep enough to ensure that, no matter how cold the winter, they will be below ice-level. Others live in large deep lakes and are assured of enough water the year round without the need to

Beaver dam

construct their complex dams. It is mainly beaver like the old fellow of this lake, living on water whose level fluctuates greatly between spring and winter, who must ensure a steady supply of water by building dams; then, when winter comes and the land around them is gripped by the great freeze, the beaver and his clan can live quietly in the water, covered by a ceiling of ice and protected from their enemies.

On this summer day the old beaver had nothing to do but eat. He was a solemn fellow, and so were his offspring, and so are all his thousands of relatives that wander through the wilderness. They take life seriously, work hard, and appear content to remain without gaiety or excitement.

In the autumn, when the leaves begin to fall and the ducks begin to gather for their trek south, the beaver and his family start providing for the long, cold winter ahead. They hew and cut and drag and carry, chopping limbs off the trees they have felled and swimming with them to their lodge area; they dive, holding the six-foot-long poles in their mouths, and finally embed them in the mud, handy to their home. By the time the first layer of ice crusts the lake, the bottom around the beaver lodge resembles a miniature forest of cut sticks and poles. All is ready for the cold.

Underwater the beaver can cut wood as easily as on land. His lips are so loose he can draw them tightly together behind his teeth. When the selected tidbit has been cut into "bedroom" length, the beaver takes it to his lodge and has his dinner, ignorant and uncaring of the elements above his head.

But this was the time of warmth and green and the beaver was not thinking of the work of autumn. After his meal on the poplar he decided to go and see what his family was doing in the den. Lazily he swam out and steered a course for home, slowly submerging his fat body some yards before reaching the small island. The entrance to the lodge was a tunnel which was nine feet long; the lodges of other beavers might have been similar, but with longer entrances, some as long as fifty feet.

Inside the lodge the family was stirring; mother, sitting near the tunnel entrance, had taken a short trip into the lake and had chewed some water lily roots for breakfast. Now she was busy with one of the combing claws beaver have on each of the two inner toes of their back feet. She had already combed herself dry, redistributing body-oil over her sleek fur, but a woody piece of lily root had embedded itself between her front teeth and she was working at this, digging it out with the special claw. She paused just long enough to make sure it was her mate in the tunnel-mouth and then continued with her task, while the young, lounging in the three-foot, oval chamber, thoroughly ignored their father.

The old beaver, likewise, ignored his family; he yawned, his shaggy countenance taking on an expression of complete boredom and, obviously hating the chore, but finding it necessary, he began combing his fur, a task which no beaver leaves undone when it returns home. Twenty minutes later he was finished and he curled himself up for a well-earned sleep while his offspring decided, one by one, to leave the lodge and seek their breakfast among the poplars.

While he slept during most of that morning hunting fangs stalked his children, one of whom, more careless than the rest, edged some distance away from the canal, aimlessly wandering in search of new food.

The lynx had been attracted here by the crashing made by the small tree the old beaver had felled. He had been too late to ambush the fat old fellow, but he had been waiting, and his patience was now rewarded. The young beaver, walking in a clumsy shuffle, headed right for the big cat which was lying behind a fallen poplar, and when the beaver was ten feet away the lynx pounced, hitting the small rodent, biting savagely at the neck. The youngster didn't even have time to scream before it died, but the noise of the attack sent the others sliding into the canal and down to the lake.

By the time the four youngsters reached the lodge their panic had gone; the parent animals eyed their children uncuriously, apparently not noticing the absence of one of them. The family settled down for another snooze, while the lynx had his first meal in three days.

This was summer, the time of plenty. Later, when the cold of winter froze the lake, the lynx would wail at the frost of night and go hungry often, while the beaver lived secure in their fortress and ate their fill.

Mother Mouse

Two beady eyes preceded by a small, pointed nose were thrust inquisitively into the green tent. Inside all was quiet and the mouse inched her furry body through the crack between the zipper and the tent bottom.

She paused, a gray blur against the opaque canvas. When she was sure the tent was empty, she scuttled over the floor and began to explore. Two beds occupied the tent. One was an iron cot, its smooth legs offering small purchase for the mouse's white feet; but the other was a camp cot, barely three inches from the ground, and one of the blankets on it had slipped off and offered easy climbing.

The mouse crept up to the blue blanket and smelled it. She took a tentative nip with her sharp teeth, pulled off a little tuft of wool and spat it out again. Then she climbed onto the bed, ran up and down it twice and settled in the center of the blanket. She worked with her teeth and her front claws, chewing at the wool, tearing it off in clumps which she left on the blanket. When she had chewed off a number of these tufts she gathered them all up in her mouth and left the tent.

Outside, the bush was black. It was the week of the waning moon and even its thin crescent was hidden by clouds. Across from the tent stood the skeleton of an unfinished cabin, its stark two-by-four bones barely visible.

The mouse crossed the twenty yards of scuffed-up ground and climbed up the floor sills. On the floor, she turned to her right, where a canvas bulged over the departed workman's tools. The mouse crawled under the canvas, guided unerringly by her keen sense of smell and the sensitive whiskers that

White-footed mouse, or deer mouse

protruded on either side of her constantly wrinkling nose.

Under the canvas was a wooden tool box equipped with one of those movable, shallow trays that sits in the top part of the box and allows room below for bulky tools. The mouse climbed the box and slid under the tray and in the darkest corner of this improvised shelter she began to build her nest. She worked all night, scurrying between the tool box and the tent, nipping and tearing at the blue blanket, pulling from it a mixture of wool and smooth rayon from the edge-binding and by morning she had constructed a fluffy ball about the size of a small melon.

An hour later, curled inside the nest, she gave birth to seven pink and wrinkled mites, each weighing about one-twelfth of an ounce. The baby mice, almost transparent, each seized on a small nipple and began feeding, and by the time they had finished their first meal their stomachs showed as minute white sacs through the thin pink skin.

The babies were born one Thursday morning in late July

and the next day the workman returned to the cabin. He lifted the canvas off the tools and dragged it outside the cabin and Mother Mouse became very agitated. She had not yet been seen, but instinct warned her that she must leave her shelter and take her babies with her.

While the workman was unpacking his car preparatory for a weekend on his property, the mouse began moving her young. Her bright eyes peered over the edge of the box as she thrust her head over, the first baby firmly but gently gripped in her mouth. The young mouse, instinctively helping his mother, had curled himself around her head.

She moved six of her babies before the workman noticed the nest. He removed the tray from the box, unintentionally dropping a hammer on the ball of blanket wool; the hammer struck the last baby mouse, injuring it and causing it to squeak. The man saw the nest and found the injured mouse. He carefully lifted the nest and the baby and placed them on the ground just outside the cabin, hoping the mother would find them and perhaps care for the youngster.

Mother Mouse did find the nest and her crying baby. Surreptitiously, she carried the youngster to the new place she had selected, the air-space in a concrete chimney block that was waiting to be used on the uncompleted cabin.

She kept her young hidden and warm during that weekend, but the chimney block wasn't really a satisfactory place for the babies. And when the man left on Sunday night, she gathered her brood together and moved them back under the canvas which the workman had again spread over his tools. But this time the mouse rebuilt her nest beside the tool box, under one flap of a cardboard box.

By the next Friday evening the injured baby had died and when the man returned the mouse was out foraging for food. The workman found the nest, carefully removed the plug of blanket with which the mouse had closed the entrance and saw the tiny, wriggling babies, now lightly clothed in a thin covering of gray-blue fur. He had just replaced the plug when the mouse returned.

Again she removed the babies from the unfinished cabin and kept them out of sight during the entire weekend,

White-footed mouse. The tip of its tail is white.

though she left the nest behind. The man, feeling sorry for the busy little mother, emptied the cardboard box, lined it with tissue and placed the empty nest in it. He had noticed that the mouse seemed able to tell when her nest was suitably located under a waterproof shelter, so when he put the box outside he first set it on a slab of wood to keep the moisture from getting in through the bottom, then he covered the top with some of the polyethylene plastic he was using to sheet the cabin. On top of all this he piled short boards, constructing a good shelter for the empty nest.

When he left on Sunday he covered the new siding boards that had been delivered the previous day with a large, black plastic sheet. He checked the nest, found it still empty and drove away, hoping the mother mouse would accept her new home.

But she didn't. As soon as the man left, Mother Mouse appeared from under the cabin, used her sharp nose to locate her empty nest and began, for the fourth time, to move it piece by piece to a location she had already selected, under the waterproof that covered the siding boards.

It took another weekend before she could be persuaded to keep her now lusty babies in the box, but eventually she took to the man-made shelter and raised her young. Twenty-one days after their birth, the little ones opened their eyes, and at two months they slipped away one by one to set up house for themselves.

The mice in our story belonged to North America's most numerous species of rodent; they are generally known as white-footed mice, but are also called deer mice, because of the similarity between their coloring and that of the white-tailed deer.

They are clean, pleasant little fellows, unlike their cousins the scavenging house mice, and they have a number of fascinating habits. Not the least of these is their song. They really do sing, producing a shrill, buzzing sound that can last for ten seconds or so.

Another unusual characteristic of this mouse is its ability to transport its young while they are still feeding on their mother's teats. The little mice set their tiny jaws in a vise-like grip on the teats and if the mother is disturbed, she just gets up and leaves her nest and babies go along, securely anchored to her stomach.

From the southland to the northern reaches of Canada, the white-footed mouse dwells in forest or in open country, raising three or four broods of young each year and providing vital food for many of the meat eaters of the wilderness. Though it is sad to think of these pretty, graceful little creatures being torn by the teeth or talons of the hunters, this is the law of the wilderness and the mice are fulfilling the part that was destined by creation to be theirs.

A Creature of Water

Winter had almost lost its grip on the land. The bush present-
ed an aspect of yellowing evergreens, bare poplars and maples, and naked willows and alders; last year's dead leaves
showed brown in open areas, soaked by the melting snow.
Under the trees, especially under the dense balsam firs, snow
huddled forlornly, as if trying to keep out of the reach of the
sun for just a little longer. Many of the birds were back now
and they were busy searching twigs and rotting timber for the
insects that were already awakening; on the ground a long-
billed, rusty woodcock strutted through the leaves, an almost
invisible, stumpy bird. Overhead the whistle of wind through
the flight feathers of mallard ducks spoke of an open lake
somewhere in the area.

The ducks came in high, flying out of the early sun. The
leader of the formation, a brilliant drake, saw the small lake
ahead and he swung the flock, circling the water before coming to land. Below the ducks the beaver pond was a mixture
of ice and floating poplar sticks, peeled of their bark by the
beaver through the winter; the water rushed towards the
dam, hit its lip and climbed over it, tumbling with a roar into
the frothy creek that traveled through the timber in twisting
course until it spent itself in a great lake many miles distant.

In the shadow of a patch of last years's cattails was a large
muskrat; except for its size and the shape of its long tail, it
looked rather like an ordinary rat as it sat munching on a section of root from a water lily. Its face was pointed and
adorned with black whiskers; its ears were small, set close to
the head. It had heavy shoulders that tapered to slim forelegs

and ended in small, agile hands. The back had a pronounced hump and seemed to rise suddenly from between the muscular haunches out of which grew the large back legs with their big, webbed feet. The rat's tail stuck out behind; it was long, black and scaly and was dressed with sparse, coarse hairs. At its root the tail was almost round, but from that point on it tapered into an oval, so that from the side it looked wide and from the top narrow.

The rat was not really hungry; it had found the bit of lily root, which had been pulled out by a beaver, and stopped to nibble on it, but it was strangely restless. This was one of last year's rats, born in its mother's second litter, and it had not felt the mating urge before. Now it was puzzled, yet powerless to prevent the urge that had brought it out of the safety of its bank burrow and its hunting territory, to wander about in search of it knew not what.

Already that morning it had stopped at every bank burrow and muskrat house it had come across, unconsciously seeking signs of a female rat; once it had found another male, like himself in search of a mate, and the two had stopped, facing each other, their strong musky odor permeating the air, and they had squeaked rage and grated their teeth in jealousy before resuming their separate journeys.

Though its coat was not now at its best, the rat was handsome; its outer fur was a rich brown, shining almost red in the April sunshine; long guard hairs gave it a rough appearance, but each time it moved the soft, silken underfur could be seen. The muskrat was large and stocky and its small eyes gave it a nearsighted appearance. In size it was about average, measuring almost twenty inches from nose to tail-tip, and weighing three pounds.

It finished the morsel of root and sat up while it cleaned its face and whiskers with its front paws; back on all fours again it moved to the lakeside and quietly slipped into the water, steering a course with its rudder-like tail for a small, untidy island that stuck out of the lake some twenty yards ahead. This was a muskrat house, a structure of sticks and dried cattail stalks and mud, rather like a beaver lodge but much smaller, which muskrats build on open water if they find a

Muskrat

place suitable for construction. The male had been born in
such a house and instinctively knew what it was, though he
had been unable to find a similar place in which to build one
for himself last autumn and had been forced to take up resi-
dence in a section of bank on the creek.

He reached the island and scrambled out of the water, his
fur glistening now more than ever. He sniffed about and the
odor of a female awoke great excitement in him; his musk
glands, two of them, hidden under the skin of his belly, discharged a few drops of oily, strong-smelling scent, his warning to any other males in the area that he would fight for the
affection of the female that lived in this house. The smell

reached the female muskrat in her house and she slipped out of her underwater entrance, emerging some yards away in deep water from where she could look at her would-be suitor. The male soon spotted her and he dived into the water, swimming strongly towards her; she evidently welcomed his attentions for she waited for him and the two swam towards the shallows, where they mated. When it was over he left her, for she now had much to do preparing for the young ones that would come within twenty-one days; and he was anxious to find another mate.

Instead he found trouble; twice he stumbled upon other males on a similar quest and they fought and their squeaks and teeth clickings filled the morning; he continued wandering for another week but was unable to find a second female willling to mate with him. This was natural, for in the muskrat world there are far more males than females and though some males manage to mate twice in one season, these are the exception.

The female muskrat was big. She was an old rat, almost five years of age, and had the male not found her when he did, she would have set out on her own, looking for a male. Now that she had mated she returned to her house and began remodeling it, repairing some of the damage done to it by the weather and by the claws of foxes and wolves which had tried to dig her out during the winter.

Muskrat lodges vary according to the age of their occupants and the time they have been living in them; usually a lodge begins as a small tent-like affair, some three feet around at the base and about two feet high. Year after year the muskrat adds to its lodge until it takes on size; and so it was with the old female's house. Now it was eight feet across at the bottom and almost four feet high and its top, instead of having the sharp peak of other years, was rounded, so that it looked rather like a strange ant-hill. Inside, the roomy chamber measured eighteen inches long by twelve inches wide and was almost a foot high; this was the female's bedroom and she could reach it through one of two entrances which were hidden under the dark waters and which led through narrow tunnels upwards, one to each end of the chamber. In one corner of the lodge was the muskrat's bed, a moist, untidy pile of cattail leaves which she had shredded with her sharp teeth, grass, and some fluffy sections of cattail heads; by human standards the rat's bed was just a soggy mess, but she did not mind it and when it got moldy she threw it out and got new bedding, though it was always wet because of its passage under the water. Spiders and numerous insects lived in the damp house and the female did not mind them either. Now and then, when summer dried its approaches, a skunk might burrow into the muddy, littered walls and live there awhile and the old rat would allow it to stay, for she was quite hospitable. At times she even shared her lodge with one of her daughters, thus it quite often served as home for two families of muskrats in a year.

There were other rat lodges on the lake. Some were even larger than the old female's and had squatted on their mud foundations for many years; around these lodges were groves of cattails, the muskrat's most important food item as well as its chief source of material for lodge construction and bedding. Near each lodge were smaller, pyramid-shaped houses, built mostly of cattail stalks. These were food shelters, for, if possible, a muskrat likes to eat in private, under cover and safe from the sudden attack of its many enemies. Usually when leaving their lodge to feed, the rats swam to their favorite cattail patch, cut a cattail and chopped it into manageable lengths with their sharp teeth; sometimes they ate them on the spot, but mostly they carried them to their feeding shelters, which floated on a raft of cattail stems.

As time wore on and the female became swollen with young, she grew bad tempered and was always ready to snap at any rats that came near her lodge. Day by day she went out less and fussed more with her bedding, until one dark night she curled up on the damp pile and started delivering her young. She had eight little ones. They were blind and almost hairless and each weighed about three-quarters of an

Muskrat house

ounce; they were almost four inches long, including their tiny, black tails. (Some muskrats have only three or four babies, others as many as eleven; usually they have between four and six.)

During the struggles of birth one of the young ones got kicked down the entrance hole and though it hung there screaming feebly for a time, the mother ignored it and it fell down the tunnel and drowned. The mother did not seem to mind; she still had seven babies left and these were enough to look after during their first week of life. By then the young had become gray-brown and wore a coat of coarse, warm hair; they moved about in the chamber, climbing over one another, but most of their time was spent drinking their mother's milk.

Sometimes muskrat young are too greedy for their own safety. They grip their mother's teats with such an iron hold that if she gets up and goes out of the den some of the youngsters are carried out with her. Blind and helpless, they float about outside crying to her and though she usually goes to them, grasping them one at a time by the slack skin on their belly and carrying them back to the lodge, it often happens that she forgets one or two, or some passing turtle may see them and snap them up.

While the female is caring for her brood, the male rat wanders aimlessly through his home territory, feeding, sleeping, and avoiding his enemies. His is a carefree life, for he has but himself to please and all day to do it in, though there is danger for him. Mink look for him almost daily, so do foxes and bobcats and lynxes and, in fact, almost every predator. Still, he survives surprisingly well and if cornered he shows plenty of courage. Standing on his powerful back legs, his short arms with their little paws held against his chest, balancing on his strong tail, he faces the enemy with long teeth bared; if the attacker is persistent the rat will utter a shrill squeak and jump for its nose, sinking his chisel teeth into it. Many a fox and mink has backed away from a determined muskrat.

Extra Teeth

Throughout the world one of the most numerous and prolific types of mammal are the fellows with the long ears, big hind legs and short, furry tails who hop about and nibble on all sorts of vegetation, transforming it into meat for the predators. Without them the eagle and the coyote, the lynx and the great horned owl, the fox and the weasel, would have a slim time of it indeed.

Until not so many years ago, hares, rabbits and pikas, with their long, chisel-like front teeth, were classified as rodents, though because they had an extra pair of smaller incisors they belonged to a special group within the order Rodentia. Some scientists, however, felt that this extra pair of teeth entitled their owners to form a separate order altogether. For many years controversy raged within the walls of biological laboratories and professors' studies and in the pages of scientific journals, and finally the "separatists" won their point. Hares, rabbits and pikas now comprise the order Lagomorpha (Greek, *lagos,* hare; *morphe,* form), and are no longer rodents.

Now, the average person can be forgiven if he thinks that this sort of re-classification smacks a little of "hare-splitting", and I am quite sure the animals themselves couldn't care less! However, this is not to belittle the efforts of taxonomists, who sort out and classify the many thousands of kinds of animals that inhabit the world today, as well as other thousands whose fossil remains tell us of their existence in past ages. Without careful organization the study of zoology would certainly be chaotic.

There is a size and style of lagomorph to suit practically

Cottontail rabbit

Nest of cottontail. The cover has been lifted to show the young rabbits.

any location in North America. We have about twenty species belonging to the order Lagomorpha; all but two of these are either hares or rabbits. The hares (*Lepus*) generally have longer ears and longer back legs; their young (called leverets) are born fully furred and with their eyes open, and are able to hop about almost as soon as they see the light of day. Our rabbits (*Sylvilagus*) are usually smaller and less powerful, hopping zigzag in the thickets and brushy areas rather than bounding vigorously over the open plains as do the hares. Rabbit babies arrive naked, blind and helpless and it is about two weeks before they reach the stage of maturity at which the hares are born.

Two kinds of pika live on this continent. They are not so closely related to the hares and rabbits as these two types of creatures are to each other; in fact, if it were not for those telltale teeth one might hardly think they were related at all. They have quite short, rounded ears and are no larger than guinea pigs; and they do not hop, but run.

Our commonest rabbit, the eastern cottontail, easily recognized by its brown coat and white, powder-puff tail, ranges from the southern parts of Ontario, Saskatchewan and Manitoba clear down to the Mexican border and below. It is between fifteen and eighteen inches long, weighs some three or four pounds, and apparently believes in producing as many young as it possibly can, bringing forth litters of four to ten, three or four times a year. In the south it breeds all the year round, but in the north, where winter shortens the breeding season, it usually compensates for the reduction in number of litters by having more young per litter.

The female eastern cottontail places her young in a fur-lined nest on the ground, in some sheltered spot. Young cottontails measure only about three inches at birth but grow to fist-size in two weeks, by which time they are well furred and start to leave the nest and nibble on green foods. At five months they are fully grown and they may mate when they are six months old, though the females usually wait some months longer.

Food for the cottontail is anything green, whether wild or cultivated, and feeding time is generally from dusk to dawn though daytime feeding is not unusual.

Counterparts of the cottontail occur in many other parts of Canada and the United States. The pygmy rabbit ranges from Nevada to southern Idaho, and from Oregon to northeastern California. It is brown-buff all over, with lighter ears that are tinged with black edges, and lacks the distinctive powder-puff of its eastern relative. It also differs from the cottontail in that it nests underground, using a burrow dug by some other animal (for, unlike European rabbits, North American rabbits do not dig their own burrows). This is the smallest of our rabbits, measuring only a foot or somewhat less.

Another interesting cottontail relative is the marsh rabbit, which likes wet places; it will swim and often dive, and likes to spend very hot days wallowing in shallow water. This rabbit is found in the southeastern part of the United States. It has thin, short, dark brown fur, and the tail is grayish on the underside. It eats mostly marsh vegetation.

Several species of hare are widely distributed over our continent. The arctic hare lives in northern Canada, Alaska and the arctic islands. It is a big animal, weighing up to twelve pounds and measuring between eighteen and thirty inches in length. For a hare, its ears are relatively short, being only three or four inches long. Those animals that live in the far north remain white all the year round, but farther south they change to brown and white in summer. This change of color is achieved by molting twice a year, not by an alteration in the pigment.

These big northerners are equipped with strong front claws with which they can dig down through hard-packed snow to find food, which consists of any kind of vegetation that can grow on the tundra. They are especially fond of the dwarf willows that grow in that region, consuming buds, leaves, twigs, bark, and even roots.

White-tailed jack rabbit

Arctic hares live most of their lives above ground and above the snow. During blizzards they may burrow into the snow for shelter, but more often they prefer to turn their backs on the biting wind and wait out the bad weather.

In the spring, at mating time, they hold large gatherings that bring perhaps forty or fifty of them together. At this time males may engage in short boxing matches, standing upright on their large hind feet and making the fur fly, though little real damage is actually done.

From two to as many as eight young are born during June and July. Only one litter is produced each year; that is all the northern climate will allow time for.

The jack rabbit is a hare with the ears of a jackass. These enormous sound scoops have the distinction of being the largest ears, in proportion to body size, of the animal world. Two species of jack rabbit commonly range through the West: the black-tailed and the white-tailed. The antelope jack rabbits, which have the largest ears of all, occur only in small numbers north of Mexico, in southern Arizona.

With their great ears and the ability to run at thirty-five miles an hour or more and cover as much as twenty feet in a single bound, the jacks are superbly adapted to survive in open country. They avoid heavy brush, which could interfere with their escape as well as providing cover for their enemies.

In wild areas, jacks are kept in check by coyotes, wolves and bobcats, as well as by eagles and the larger hawks and owls; snakes are an additional hazard for the small leverets. But in settled places, where man has gone to a great deal of trouble to kill off most of the predators, the jacks multiply unchecked and become the farmer's greatest pest, consuming large amounts of alfalfa and other cultivated crops. Then man declares war on the big hares, and becomes their greatest enemy.

The black-tailed jack rabbit is found from South Dakota to the Pacific coast and southward into Mexico. Its coat is brownish-gray on the back and sides, and white underneath. Its tail is black on the upper surface.

Pika

The white-tailed jack rabbit ranges somewhat farther north, from Saskatchewan to New Mexico, and west into the Cascades and Sierras, where it is sometimes found as high as 10,000 feet. Unlike the black-tailed species, which remains brown all year, in the northern part of its range the white-tailed jack rabbit turns pure white in the wintertime.

Jack rabbits can weigh up to eight or ten pounds and measure more than two feet in length. The female is usually larger than the male.

The pika dwells in colonies in high mountain country and prefers rough, scree-laden faces where there are plenty of nooks and crannies into which to duck when threatened by hawks and other predators. He will also burrow holes for himself.

This plump little animal measures between six and eight inches in length and weighs little more than six ounces at most.

He is covered with warm gray-brown fur that makes him hard to spot in his rocky habitat. There is fur even on the soles of his feet, enabling him to leap from rock to rock without losing his footing.

The pika is a busy little chap and a great farmer, gathering hay which he spreads out to cure in the sun before storing it in his burrow for winter use. If it should rain, he carries his hayrack to shelter, then brings it out again when the rain is over. When it is completely cured, he stashes it away below ground. In the winter he does not hibernate, but pops up and down through the snow, assured of food by his store of hay.

In a nest under the rocks the three or four young are born between late May and early September. Weighing hardly more than a third of an ounce, they are born furred and with their eyes open, and are soon able to manage on their own.

The great grizzly bear loves to dig out pikas and evidence of a bear's dig is easy to spot. I once saw a crater in which a small automobile could have been hidden and I am yet at a loss to know why a grizzly would bother to do so much digging for such a little meal!

This Machine Will Self-Destruct

The lemming is a rodent, the snowshoe hare is a lagomorph, biological names that tell us that each of these mammals belongs to a separate order. If they are viewed side by side, there is little physical resemblance between them, yet they are linked by one important characteristic: each has inherited a built-in mechanism for self-destruction. The lemming self-destructs by running itself to death; the snowshoe hare worries itself into a total nervous breakdown that persists until the animal simply dies.

Until recent times there was no certain explanation for the strange behavior of these two animals, although their cycles of abundance and scarcity have been recognized for a great many years. For centuries man has known that the lemmings go on seemingly pointless mass migrations approximately every four years, but it was not until the Hudson's Bay Company became established in Canada that the snowshoe hare's unusual fluctuations were noted. Records kept by the fur-trading company showed that the hares have a ten-year cycle, increasing normally for several years then undergoing a sudden population explosion for the next two or three years, followed by a drastic decline. For example, in 1845 some 20,000 snowshoe hare pelts were traded at Hudson's Bay Company posts; three years later the number of pelts declined to about 10,000, but by 1853 almost 90,000 pelts were received.

Because many other fur-bearing animals feed on the snowshoe—such as the lynx, fox, mink, wolverine and weasel —hare populations were of vital interest to the fur traders as

Collared, or varying lemming

valuable furs became plentiful or scarce according to the fluctuations in number of the snowshoe hare. Thus, after some years, the hare's unexplained peaks and valleys of population were referred to as "the fur cycle".

Today we are beginning to understand some of the reasons for the population cycles of both the hare and the lemming, though few books so far written about wildlife for the layman explain the interesting mechanics of their decline.

Humans in today's society are becoming aware of the problems that arise from stuffing a large number of people into a limited land area, but most sociologists appear to believe that the resulting ills are uniquely human in origin. Not so! The manifestations of human overcrowding may indeed be unique in that people use unnatural "aids" to deal with their frustrations; drugs and alcohol are but two examples of this.

In the wild the stresses of crowding are the same—but

there are no unnatural aids. Nature, whose purpose is always the perpetuation of the species rather than the welfare of the individual, recognizes the threat of overpopulation. Just as too few of one kind of animal will lead to its extinction, too many of a species can result in the disappearance of its own kind and of many other forms of life—even of *all* life, if that species happens to be man!

For these reasons nature built into the scheme of things certain safety factors—predators, disease, and so on—that work for the good of the species as a whole. To attempt to describe all of the many and varied ways by which balance is maintained in natural populations would be far beyond the scope of this chapter. We can, however, begin to examine the peculiar mechanism which operates to ensure stability among the lemmings and the snowshoe hares, and consequently among a host of other species that either depend upon them for food or require the living space that would be threatened by an overabundance of one or the other.

Three species of lemming inhabit the far northern regions of North America—the brown, the bog and the collared lemming. All are small, chunky, short-tailed animals that live in underground "cities", making a network of tunnels beneath the arctic tundra. The brown lemmings normally produce two litters of five or six between April and September; the collared are known to breed throughout the year.

Food for the lemmings is any kind of vegetable or seed that grows in their range, some of which is eaten in the open while some is taken into the underground nest for storage. (Recently Canadian scientists discovered a cache of food that had been put away by some lemming of prehistory; the seeds were taken to the Central Experimental Farm in Ottawa, where they were planted and grew into a type of plant long extinct in the world!)

The snowshoe hare is a hard animal to spot at any time of year because its coat changes from brown to white with the seasons. It freezes like a statue when merely startled, but when it is seriously alarmed it is one of the fastest animals in

Varying hare, snowshoe hare or snowshoe rabbit

the forest; it has actually been clocked at speeds up to thirty miles an hour and can leap as much as twelve feet in one bound. Snow does not hamper its progress as its big hind feet with their spreading toes are covered with fur on the underside, forming efficient "snowshoes" with which the animal can travel over the surface of even the softest snow with ease.

This common hare ranges throughout North America, south of the tree line, keeping mostly to wooded country. Mating begins in spring and the young are born some thirty-six days later. The average number of young per litter is four, but as few as two and as many as six or seven may be born, in a well-camouflaged grass nest that is built on the ground, in some slight hollow or depression. Like all young hares, the snowshoes are fully furred when born, their eyes are open, and they are able to hop about within a short time of birth. At first they usually remain in the nursery unless they are disturbed, suckled by their mother during periodic visits to her brood, usually at night; but within three or four weeks the young are fending for themselves. A female snowshoe hare will have several litters of young each year.

While the snowshoe hares go about the business of "dying off" in a less spectacular, though equally effective, manner, the lemmings, when they become too numerous, run to their death in grandstand migrations. Thousands upon thousands pour from their overcrowded burrows and head off in any direction, running until they are picked off by predators or collapse from exhaustion, not even stopping when they reach the sea or some other body of water; then they just swim until they drown. Of course, while the hordes race off to die, there are always some who stay behind, ensuring continuation of the species in their area, where the numbers slowly build up until the next population explosion starts the whole thing going once again.

Now, what causes these animals to disregard the precepts of safety and virtually to commit suicide?

Countless survival factors operate within the scheme of nature, but one important trait is shared by all animals: the response to alarm. This is caused by a series of complex chemical reactions that enable prey or predator to respond quickly to alarm with action, providing emergency forces that help it to escape, or to chase and attack. In warm-blooded animals, the heart beats faster because more blood is needed to operate the muscles; the breathing accelerates because there is extra blood to purify; the "action" muscles, such as those of the legs, back, shoulders and feet, become more blood-absorbent so that they can accommodate the additional supplies sent to them by heart and lungs; while muscles that are not important for running or for fighting, such as the stomach muscles, contract (this accounts for the feeling of "butterflies in the stomach" experienced in the face of shock or fear).

This "alarm response" is nature's way of helping the cause of survival under normal conditions, but it is also a means of thinning down the ranks of a species that has overpopulated itself! What are the factors that trigger the physical changes needed to respond to alarm? Not all of them are yet known, but some are and they appear to be the most important.

Certain endocrine glands, particularly the pituitary and the adrenal, discharge into the bloodstream of an animal in the grip of alarm particular hormones that immediately go to work, causing the physical changes described. The pituitary gland, located in the brain, manufactures some five distinct hormones that control water metabolism, blood pressure, the function of the kidneys and the smooth working of the muscles; the adrenal glands discharge a hormone called adrenalin, which appears to be the trigger of the alarm reaction. Both glands, working in unison, combine to give the alarmed animal a powerful "shot in the arm" by putting into its bloodstream relatively large amounts of the hormones that are discharged in smaller quantities during normal times.

We see from this that although the endocrine glands are always releasing hormones into the bloodstream, the output is stepped up in times of stress. Provided that the state of alarm is genuine, these extra quantities of hormones serve a necessary purpose and cause no ill effects because they are "burned up" through physical action. But if the state of alarm is induced, not by actual physical danger but by forces that simply get on the animal's nerves, the glands, while they do not discharge as much of their various hormones as they would in face of a genuine alarm, still release more than the usual amounts for normal body function. But as the false alarm is not followed by violent activity the extra adrenalin and other hormones in the bloodstream are not burned off in the normal way; thus, if the cause of the false alarm remains and the nervous animal continues fretting for a long time, eventually something must give. As with an internal combustion engine that is fed too much gasoline, the vital parts of the animal's body come to a halt, flooded by hormones!

This is what happens to the snowshoe hare when it overpopulates itself. Overcrowding, resulting in intense competition for food and shelter, brings about a state of continuous alarm, and the animals literally worry themselves to death. The poor hares go into a nervous decline and finally there comes a complete metabolic breakdown and they die.

Lemmings, on the other hand, when they reach the breaking point, react physically and dramatically. Breeding stops and they erupt from their overcrowded cities and run insanely to their death.

We are beginning to understand a little about nature's ways of regulating animal populations, and eventually, through the patient efforts of scientists throughout the world, we shall understand a great deal more. In the meantime, there is much about which we can only speculate. What causes the sudden increase in population of some species? Why do lemmings, which normally produce two litters of five or six a year, produce double that number of litters and as many as eight young per litter in the summer preceding their great migration? Why do peak years of lemming or hare often coincide with peak years for other entirely unrelated species, such as shrews, or certain kinds of moths and butterflies whose larvae when overabundant strip whole forests of their leaves? These are questions for which there are as yet no certain answers.

The Howling Pack

The ululating cry filled the dawn with sadness. It began with quick, staccato yelps, hesitated, then launched into a wild contralto.

From far away, softly and indistinctly at first, came the answer. The long, moaning howl floated alone among the spruce trees, reaching the young wolf where he sat, squatted on lithe haunches atop a pinnacle of snow-crusted granite. Before the answering call ended the young wolf whined excitement; he sat still, holding his head to one side, making cups of his ears, and as he listened he smiled, showing the long, curved fangs that framed the cavity of his pink mouth.

The glossy black fur that protected the young wolf from the cold of this February day showed that this animal had withstood exceptionally well the rigors of a northwoods winter. He was a three-year-old, an eager, brash young male who was now, for the first time in his short life, setting out to find himself a mate.

Filled with the restlessness that grips his kind between January and March, when the mating call is strongest, he had left his family the week before to roam alone through the forest, seeking the mate who would probably become his lifetime companion and mother to several generations of stubby, vibrant pups. He had traveled far, stopping often to examine the tracks of other packs, following them for a time, then turning away as some stronger and more compelling scent drove him in a new direction.

Twice in the week he had turned aside from his search to hunt for meat, but even after the kill, when with bulging stomach he would have settled for a long sleep under ordinary conditions, he had continued trotting tirelessly through the evergreens, stopping often to launch his sad love song, listening for an answer and not receiving one, until now.

The wolf waited for the distant call to end; when stillness engulfed the bush, he sat straight, pointed his broad head towards the incarnadine sky and launched again his plaintive call over the tree-tops. The cry lasted for perhaps fifteen seconds and when it stilled, the young wolf rose and bounded off the rock, down into the forest and away, running swiftly towards the east on a course that would unerringly intercept the female that had answered his wild call.

The black wolf was big, almost as husky as his arctic cousins, which may scale 120 pounds and more; fully matured and in perfect condition, the youngster weighed over 100 pounds and had an exceptionally massive head equipped with jaws so powerful they could snap the heavy leg bones of deer or elk. His coloring, though darker than that of most of his brothers and sisters, was not uncommon among timber wolves.

This morning, as the wolf ran through stands of spruce and tamarack and forced his way under and over barriers of leafless brush, he stopped often along his way at certain spots in the forest. These were scent stations, haphazardly selected places where, during mating time, wolves deposit a drop or two of their urine to let others of their kind know that they have passed this way. These places and their scents tell the age, sex and other characteristics of each wolf to the newcomer, who, after he has read the sign of others, deposits his own personal message.

Under different circumstances the black wolf would have lingered over the smells at each scent station, but now, on his way to meet the bitch he hoped would become his mate, he took only enough time to give a hasty sniff or two and deposit his own scent, then he ran on, guided by the blind instinct all animals possess, on a completely unknown course through the high timbers to meet the stranger that had lured him with her deep, throaty call.

He stopped suddenly, his big head held high, his ears

pricked forward. The sounds that reached him would have been inaudible to a man, but they told him that perhaps half a mile ahead there was a pack of wolves. When he set off again he altered his style of travel; before he had run swiftly, incautiously, without heed of the noise he was making; now he traveled with stealth, gliding shadow-like through the bush, placing his feet with care, his body held low and his eyes constantly probing the terrain.

Soon he smelled the others and their noise became louder. He stopped and scanned the country around him. The tall evergreens had given way to muskeg cedar, gnarled, bushy trees that hid much from sight with their dark green boughs that swept down to ground level; but the keen eyes of the black wolf spotted movement about 100 yards ahead, where gray shapes slipped back and forth under the branches.

He watched a moment longer, his big body almost totally hidden by a deadfall, then he leaped over the rotting tree and whined loudly. At once there was silence from the wolf family ahead. The black wolf advanced a few paces, stopped and sat on his haunches, holding himself tall; he whined again and waited. The pack bunched together and watched the newcomer, warily, suspicious of everything about this stranger that was intruding on the family.

The leader of the pack, father and grandfather to nine of the eleven wolves that made up the family, took two steps away from the others and stood alone, a shaggy, battle-scarred veteran of twelve winters, and as he stood there his lips curled in a silent snarl that showed the razor-like teeth that might yet repel the cheeky visitor; the black wolf whined again, wagged his bushy tail and moved forward slowly, telling the old warrior as plainly as he could that he came in friendship. The old wolf let him come and the pack opened to receive him.

Now he was ringed by the wolves. Five of them were pups, born the previous spring, but still large and equipped with fighting fangs. Apart from them and the old wolf, there were two mature males and two females and, the black wolf saw with excitement, one other female, a young she-wolf who stood a little away from him, eyeing him expectantly.

Timber wolf, howling

The black wolf grinned at her and made to move in her direction and the whole pack, including the object of his search, fell upon him, rolling him over and over on the ground and snapping at his legs and body.

He made no effort to protect himself. He had often taken part in similar displays, when other lone wolves had come courting one of his own kind. He knew that the pack would either rough him up a little, to see if he was worthy to mate with their relative, or they would become vicious and kill him, if he didn't escape. Only the whim of the old leader would decide which it was to be, and the black wolf waited, braving the storm of snarls and bites, but ready to jump up and escape if he should have to.

As suddenly as the pack had attacked, it withdrew, and the black wolf rose to his feet. Now all the wolves except the young female went about their business; they had accepted the stranger and there was no more to be said or done, so they ignored him.

Not so the young female. She pranced towards the black wolf and bit him on the shoulder, playfully, taking care not to hurt, then she ran from him only to stop a few yards away and look at him over her shoulder. The black wolf whined and ran after her and the two of them disappeared into the forest.

At that moment the young wolf became the leader of a pack; it was a pack of two now but in May, some sixty-three days after he mated with the female, six or eight pups would be born in some cave or badger burrow she would choose as her family's first home, and the pack would be complete, the family social unit which is so important in the wolf world.

From now on, both the black wolf and his gray mate, powerful, savage killers of almost every living creature, including at times their own kind, would be devoted parents, more kindly towards their scampering cubs than any other wild animal toward its young. Mother, so bloodthirsty on the hunt, would become an affectionate slave to her brood, and the black wolf would be patient, docile and big-hearted with his sons and daughters.

He would teach them to hunt, taking them first on short forays around the den, preparing them for maturity, when they would follow hunting routes for 100 miles and more perhaps twice each month. He would teach them how to run down the fleetest game, like deer, moose or caribou, trotting behind them for tireless hours at a patient, determined pace of some twenty miles an hour, much slower than the game they were chasing, but of incredible endurance which eventually would tire the quarry, leaving the wolves still fresh and able to put on a final spurt of speed, lunge quickly against the exhausted animal and knock it to the ground. After that, two or three powerful, slashing bites with the keen fangs and the kill would be made.

So they would live out their time in the wilderness, wild, free and savage, killing and perhaps being killed, but royal in their existence, as untamed as they were in primordial times, the howling, vibrant pack.

The Night Raiders

The spruce forest is a pleasant place of dappled sun and thick carpets of springy brown needles; it is a place of quiet footsteps, of low rustling sounds, of soft calls. The fresh trees grow tall and straight and scent the air with their fragrance, for it is summer and the sap is running again through the scaly skin that covers each spruce. Red squirrels race through the upper reaches of the forest, nibbling at the green buds or picking off the warm brown cones; jays screech at each other and the soft call of a ruffed grouse comes from under a big old tree. Beneath the layers of dry needles there is red earth, soft and moist; lush earth that nourishes the yellowish roots of the trees and the bushes and the small, lovely wild flowers that grow in sunny places. The land rolls, climbing several feet at times; it also dips, forming hollow places here and there.

On the bare side of a low hill there is a group of granite rocks, five gray masses of stone clustered together. Beneath one of these boulders young life is frisking exuberantly as seven coyote pups engage in a mock battle. They look like collie dog puppies, except that they are gray in color and have a certain lush and alertness not given to domestic creatures; they have big, pointed ears which stand straight up and are always on the move, scooping sounds out of the air; they have small brown eyes, clear and intelligent, smiling eyes now, for they are at play; they have long, bushy tails and this is what they are chasing, each trying to grasp the other's so that they gallop, run and jump in a rough circle, like children playing ring-a-roses.

Coyote

Mother sits above them, eyeing them with pride. She has a short body, the bushy tail of her kind, a gray coat which is not as sleek and shiny as those of her pups. She sits on her haunches. Her belly fur is white, her sides are tawny and there are a few splashes of black almost hidden under the gray on her back; she has a long muzzle and black lips which are parted, allowing her long, pink tongue to escape and hang over the side of her lower jaw. Her white teeth shine under the early June sunlight and her limp tongue quivers jerkily as she takes short, panting breaths.

The red earth shows fresh scars at the base of the rock upon which the coyote bitch sits, for it is there that the mother burrowed, carving a shelter for herself and the pups she was carrying; that was five weeks ago, just before April gave way to May. Shortly before the small she-wolf dug her den a handsome male ran with her, but when the time of birth drew near the bitch told him to go, and he left her, though never going far from the lair of his mate. He hunted more

94

now and came often to the birth place and each time he dropped meat outside its entrance; hares, mice, grouse, carrion, anything that would feed his mate while she waited for her young to come.

One morning, early, before the sun climbed above the darkness, the male trotted up the slope with the body of a woodchuck in his mouth; a bright moon had come last night and the marmot, lured from the safety of its earth home, was feeding on tender grasses when the coyote pounced; now it was to serve as breakfast for the bitch wolf and the male was proud of his hunt. As he dropped the carcass at the accustomed place, just outside the den entrance, the coyote froze, his ears pricking forward. From somewhere in the earth faint cries reached him. His children had come at last.

He stood outside listening for several minutes and once he whined eagerly, but he did not go in, for this was forbidden. This ban would continue until the cubs were five weeks old and able to scamper about outside. Meanwhile the male would hunt for himself and for his mate and for his seven children, seeking no favors and uncomplaining.

Coyotes are small, slender wolves, a separate species and different in many ways from their relatives, the timber wolves. Whereas timber wolves can weigh as much as 120 pounds, the little brush wolf hardly tips the scales past the thirty-pound mark as a rule, though some of the bigger males have been known to double that weight.

The name by which they are popularly known was first given to them by the Aztec Indians of Mexico; they christened them *coyotl*, and then came the Spaniards and adopted the Indian name, giving it a pronunciation of their own which has endured to the present time.

Like the timber wolves, coyotes usually mate for life; sometimes a "divorce" between a male and female may take place one year or so after the first mating, but these instances are rare and death is the most common cause of separation.

In the West, where cattle, sheep and chickens are raised in thousands by the ranchers, the coyote is hated by the stockmen, who never miss a chance to kill him. Often a devoted father wolf will give his life so that his mate and young may live; this happens when a hunter, out looking for the lair, gets too close to it. The male, knowing that something must be done to distract the enemy, slips out of the den and darts into the open, leading the hunter away. Sometimes, if the country is rough or heavily wooded, the male returns home several hours later after shaking off his pursuer, but all too often the gallant little wolf is shot to death, or run down by the hunter's jeep as he races at speeds up to twenty-five miles an hour across open land, dodging frantically in his attempts to elude the roaring monster that is chasing him.

The small wolf is extremely intelligent and daring and he is one of the few wild animals that thrives side by side with civilization; while most creatures flee to the wilderness when man settles an area, the coyote, like the skunk, stays on and prospers, using man in order to enjoy an easy living. But though he is a killer of sheep and chickens and calves, there is a good side to the brush wolf; he is the garbage man of the wilds and cleans up after other predators, consuming quickly that which death has left behind. Marshes and streams would soon become polluted with carrion without him, and mice, rats and other rodents harmful to the farmer's grain are devoured in their hundreds every summer by the coyote. But it is always difficult to persuade an angry farmer that the wolf which has just killed one of his sheep is only taking payment for a job well done! Even so, it seems that the cunning little wolves are here to stay; they are more than a match for the stockmen and despite poisoning and trapping and shooting, there are more coyotes today than there were twenty years ago, and they are spreading into areas where they were never seen in the past.

This may be because coyotes are prolific breeders and make good parents and maintain definite territories for themselves. A pair will stake out an area in which there is enough game to sustain the father and mother and their young while these are growing up; once the cubs reach maturity, however, they must leave home and seek their own hunting grounds, or they and their parents would quickly kill off all the game.

In this way each young wolf goes out into the world, finds a home and eventually settles down with another of the opposite sex to raise young of their own.

Mating takes place during January, February and part of March and a noisy time it is, too; the coyotes become restless and excited and night after night launch their yipping cry to the moon and the stars. Theirs is a shriller, more musical note than the big timber wolf's baying howl and often two or three coyotes will sing a chorus, apparently in deliberate performance.

When the singing is over and after some of the males have been involved in fierce, bloody fights, it is the female that chooses her mate—and often the contrary lady chooses the defeated wolf! As few as three and as many as eighteen cubs are born to the she sixty-three days after mating takes place and this is the busiest time for the father, who hunts for them all. The little ones at birth are blind and almost hairless, except for a coating of fine hair and they look in shade and size like a litter of puppies sired by a domestic dog.

A blood moon hangs in the sky. The spruce forest is a place of many shadows and quiet, rustling sounds; now and then a great horned owl hoots at the night as he sits in seeming boredom on a branch in a big spruce. Outside the coyote den the family is gathered; the mother is lying on her side and one of her sons is pulling at her tail. The others are frisking just inside the den mouth while the male wolf sits on his haunches, testing the night air with his sensitive nose. The cubs are two months old and the male has been allowed to return to the den, for he must start to teach his children how to hunt.

The male seems to make up his mind about something. He rises to all fours, gives one last look at the moon and then turns to his mate; she has been watching him and seems to be ready, for the moment his head turns she jumps to her feet, sending the cub tumbling over himself. The father whines once and immediately the cubs stop whatever they are doing and rush to him, clustering around him in great excitement.

Earlier this evening he played with the little ones, joining in their rough-and-tumble games, now he disdains them and trots slowly into the spruce forest. The young ones know. This is to be a hunting night and they can hardly restrain themselves as they scamper gleefully after their sire, followed more cautiously by the mother. All night they stay out and mostly they get in the way as father or mother shows them where to find snowshoe hares or ruffed grouse, or how to pounce on a scurrying mouse, but they learn, too, and three of them catch mice. By morning, when the sun starts cutting into the night, the family returns to the den for a sleep that may last a few hours or the entire day.

From now on the cubs will be kept busy and playtime will be limited, for they must learn the art of hunting before the first crisp winds of autumn come to warn of the snow and cold that is ahead. Fortunately, hunting comes naturally to the young wolves and their insatiable appetite dictates that anything is food; throughout the year, their diet includes birds, squirrels, mice, carrion, anything vegetable when they feel like it, fruit, frogs, beetles, fish, muskrats, beaver, deer, and even porcupines, despite the great danger of the slow-moving animal's quills.

But today the cubs are still carefree as they sleep curled into little round balls deep inside their den. Outside the sun is high over the spruce forest and the birds and small creatures are out again, feeding each in its own way, calling to one another, making the music of the wilderness, for night is still a long way off and most of the predators are asleep.

Cunning Hunter

A black nose tapers from a sharp muzzle; two brown, intelligent eyes and two pointed, inquisitive ears show through an opening in the long grass; reddish whiskers, fine and shiny in the early morning light, quiver slightly as the fox's breath escapes through his nostrils. The eyes, steady and full of curiosity, survey a green, rolling clearing that is rich with the scent of budding clover; the lush field is part of a farm that was once carved out of the wilderness and has long ago been abandoned because the farmer was too far from markets and his life was too hard here on the edge of the backwoods. But the field is still productive, although the clover is thinner now and wild plants mix with it, such as golden mustard and bright sow thistles and wild daisies, with their white petals and dusty yellow hearts.

The red fox remains still, a breathing statue whose body is concealed by the grass that grows on the north edge of the clearing; he is listening, sitting on his haunches, waiting to hear again the tiny rustling sound that stopped him as he was about to break through into the field. He knows that small sound; it was made by a meadow mouse pattering through a tunnel, the roof of which is formed by a mat of old clover and grass, partly mulched now, running just above the roots of the growing plants; the floor of the tunnel is the brown earth, beaten hard by the feet of the tiny rodents as they slip from one part of the field to another.

The small noise is repeated, not far away, only a few yards over there, by the clump of slowly-waving daisies. The red fox moves. He moves slowly, face eager, feet highstepping as

Red fox at den entrance

his black legs scissor one in front of the other. Patiently he
stalks the sound, knowing that the little creature that made it
is now still, quaking under its flimsy covering, for it has
heard the stealthy approach of the fox and now sits immobile,
hoping that the enemy will miss its hiding place.

For a fraction of time the red fox pauses, bushy tail with its
white tip held high, one front leg up and curled under, in the
act of coming down; then he pounces, using his haunches to
lift himself up and forward, coming down first with his front
paws, pushing at the grass, feeling for the life he knows is
there. He misses, pounces again, and again, and this time the
paws trap the escaping mouse and the fox's quick muzzle dips

down and up and the mouse is caught between the white teeth, dead. In a trice the rodent is eaten and the fox continues on his way, quartering the clearing, looking for more mice, occasionally stopping to nibble at the clover. Before another hour is done he has caught and eaten five mice and he is satisfied but thirsty as he lopes away, a shiny, glossy red in the sunlight, his handsome "brush" waving like a flag.

At a small beaver pond the fox stops to drink; he crouches, leaning over the muddy bank, stretching his neck to the water, and his tongue comes out and forms a drinking cup; he laps water into his mouth, his quick eyes searching the area ahead just in case there is something more to eat or something to be feared. After the drink he sits up on his haunches, the favorite stance of all foxes, and he licks his lips and the fur around his mouth. Somewhere up on his right shoulder a louse is sucking his blood. A black hind leg comes up and curled toes with their stubby, short claws scratch quickly at the itch. A few hanks of whitish-brown fur fly off and are caught by the breeze and draped over the fluffy end of a cattail.

It is time for sleep. The fox turns his back on the pond and trots towards the forest, seeking a place of concealment in which to lie and doze until hunger again drives him to look for food. The young male, or "dog", stands fifteen inches high at the shoulder and measures three feet in length. He weighs eleven pounds, a good weight for a red fox. Last February he mated with the vixen of his choice and the two settled down in a den that they dug in a soft sand bank near a tumbling brook; they made their own home this time, because the digging was easy, but in other years, with other mates, the vixen looked for an abandoned skunk or porcupine burrow that could be enlarged, for these slim foxes are poor diggers.

One night in March, when the vixen who was to be his partner for the rest of this year was already beginning to bulge with young, the two were late returning to their lair; the hunt had been a poor one and they had searched until almost dawn before their hunger was satisfied. They were walking in single line, the vixen leading along an indistinct trail through the forest, when something snapped at her from the ground. She had stepped into a spring trap set by a man last winter and forgotten, but still deadly as it skulked under its covering of earth and leaves.

The iron jaws gripped the vixen high up the left foreleg and though she pulled mightily the jaws would not set her free. Terror filled both animals. The dog tried to help his mate bite the iron, but at last, two hours later, there was only one thing to do and the vixen did it. She lay on the trail and patiently chewed through the flesh and sinews and bone of her leg, above where it was held by the cruel vise; at last she was free, but blood rushed from her maimed limb as she staggered with her mate to the den. Infection set in three days later and the vixen died, and the dog left the den forever.

Because it was past the mating season the fox would wander alone for the rest of the year, waiting for a new February, when he would seek another mate with whom he would stay until the next winter came, helping her to hunt for the litter of new cubs and teaching the little foxes the ways of the forest. Then, when the cubs were old enough to go into the world, the dog and the vixen would separate, perhaps to meet and mate again, perhaps not.

Born four years earlier in an old marmot burrow, the fox was one of a litter of six. He resembled his father; his coat on the back and sides and most of his brush were a deep chestnut-red. His underside was white, like the tip of his tail, and his legs, from the knees and elbows down to the feet, were black. His mother was of the same species, but her coloring was glossy ebon that shone when sunlight caught the gleam of long, white-tipped guard hairs, she was what is known as a silver fox. Among the red fox's brothers and sisters there were two kits like the mother, one which did not resemble either parent, being a mixture of both, and three, including the dog, like the father. Such mixing of colors is common in red fox families. Predominantly they are red, but many of them are black or a mixture of black, yellow and red.

The red fox was one of an average litter; some vixens have only four kits, others as many as nine. The young arrive fifty-one days after the mating, usually towards the end of March or the beginning of April. They are pretty little creatures, like small puppies, each about three inches long, almost hairless and blind, but already they have those sharp noses and the triangular ears and the tail hair is heavier than on the body. Five weeks later they are little square things, fat and playful as they leave their den to romp within reach of the safety of their home, which usually has four or five entrances.

The kits roll and tumble and wrestle each other, gaining strength and sureness of movement and practicing the quickness which one day will help them secure their food. As they scamper about outside they seem careless of danger, but centuries of self-preservation have placed in even such small and helpless things an alertness that never relaxes. Their biggest danger outside the den is the gliding, rapacious eagle that can see a moving mouse a mile away, and now and then one of the little foxes looks up to the sky, searching for the dreaded shape.

Life was uneventful for the red fox and his brothers and sisters. At first their father hunted for the whole family, bringing food twice a day for them when the milk of their mother no longer satisfied their growing appetites. By late summer they were old enough to go out with their parents and learn how to hunt for themselves and learn, too, of the dangers that lurked in the great green world in which they lived. Even in that wilderness there was man, with his traps and snares; and there were the big timber wolves, and their smaller cousins, the coyotes, and the fierce lynx, and the bobcat. But a healthy, adult fox fears little if he has learned well his lessons as a cub.

Nature has equipped the fox for survival where other things perish. In the domain of man, where the red fox lives and is as much at home as in the great wilderness, the cunning little hunter seems actually to enjoy pitting his sharp wits against those of the hunter and his dogs, laying a series of complicated trails, crossing over logs, jumping great distances, and doubling back on his tracks to confuse the pack. In the wilderness, pitted against his natural foes, the fox is always alert, cautious and quick to escape. And yet he is a friendly fellow, this red fox. Often he will go up to young deer and play with them, if they will let him. He is curious, especially of man; he will come into the open to inspect a woodsman and can be lured close by even the most clumsy imitations of his high-pitched scream, the call to his mate. But for all that, he is evasive, quick to leap away and as intelligent as they come.

When the red fox was starting his second year and had already found a mate, he was out alone one evening, seeking food, when the trail led him to a river. From the other side he heard the high-pitched whistle of a woodchuck; over there, across the water, was food for the taking, if he was patient enough. Swimming has no terrors for the fox; his woolly coat, trapping air, makes him buoyant and with his body high in the water he can swim long distances. Tonight, using great caution, he slipped into the river and swam quietly to the other side. Soon he located the woodchuck burrows, but the timid creatures had disappeared; he settled to wait for them. He knew that sooner or later one of those fat woodchucks would creep out of its den to feed on the tender grasses of spring. He lay on his belly for almost an hour, still as a log, unblinking, and finally his patience was rewarded. A quick run and a lightning snap of the sharp teeth and a plump marmot was dead, a good meal for his mate waiting in the lair for the coming of her young.

That winter, after he had parted from the vixen and his children, the red fox almost lost his life. It was December and the snow was not deep yet and he was following grouse tracks when he heard a vicious snarl. He was startled, for his always alert senses had not detected any signs of danger; the noise came from under a downed tree. The dog looked hard and suddenly he saw another of his kind, a thin, ragged animal lying on its side under the ancient pine. The fox felt uneasy in the presence of this stranger and edged away, towards the heavy bush, where there was shelter, and it was well that he did. The strange fox rose and from its open mouth white froth came and saliva dripped from its jaws; there was a crazed look in the brown eyes. Instinct made the dog run away from this place, and he escaped with his life, for the strange fox was gripped by the virus that drives things mad —rabies.

At times, when fox populations are high, the dreaded disease comes to them and the creatures die horribly, often infecting other animals as they run madly through the forest, biting at anything, living or dead. This sickness is the biggest enemy of foxes and other creatures of the wild, for the terror spreads wide in wintertime, even to man and his domestic animals.

Giant of the North

Far to the north, beyond the tree line, there is a land of ice and leaden seas and howling winds of death. It is a place of pack ice and bergs, of short, dusky men and sleek white whales, a world of seals and walruses, of ptarmigan and snow hares. It lies glistening, cold, mysterious, unchanged by age or man, at times so silent that life would seem to have ceased upon its surface, at other times launching its many voices in haunting melodies that dance over the icefields; the low, moaning call of the great tundra wolf, the hoarse bark of the seal, the primordial scream of the north wind.

This is the roof of the world, a vast and lonely tract that has taken good men and killed them and has touched others and marked them forever, because man, despite the superiority of his intellect, is the weakest being in that circle of arctic white. Yet he has survived, using cunning and guile to defeat the elements, and this is as much his story as the story of a gigantic yellowish bear that pads impervious over the snow and ice, swimming from berg to island, from island to mainland, pausing now and then to smell the country, his big head swinging from side to side as though keeping time with a rhythm that only his own short ears can detect.

The polar bear was stalking a seal. It was December, and the morning was young. Out on the thick ice that framed the north end of Bathurst Island, where the salty waters of Melville Sound flow to meet the Beaufort Sea, the polar bear was trying to focus his eyes on a distant mark, darker than the white ice, which, he thought, might be the blow-hole of a seal. He was a big bear, a shaggy, powerful male who had

Polar bears

been made more than usually savage that day because of the
emptiness that was in his belly. The wind came from the
west, blowing across his front, useless because it would not
carry to him the smells that lurked over the dark patch of ice.
Peering harder, but still unable to pierce the distance, he
grunted in anger and began to move with the wind, padding
towards the east, intent on circling the dark patch until he
met the wind head-on, so that it could tell him what he
would find out there. Seals are quick, alert creatures and the
bear, an experienced hunter, knew that he must first explore
the dark patch with his keen nose, keeping away from it, out

of sight and smell of the seal, until he was in position to make his lightning lunge before the amphibian mammal could escape through the blow-hole.

Half a mile behind the bear, on the island, there was a rise of land. Behind this, crouched so that only the top of his head and his eyes appeared over the rim, was a man. He was watching the bear. He clutched a short spear and a knife was strapped around his waist, over the thick fur parka he was wearing. A leather loop passed around his neck, over his shoulder and down under his left arm; the ends of the loop were fastened to a walrus-skin bag that rested against his back. He was short and stocky and he had wide shoulders. Drab mukluks encased his legs and feet; mitts of sealskin kept the cold from his hands; and his broad face with the high cheek-bones and squat nose was almost hidden by the hood of a parka that was rimmed outside with the fur of a wolf, which does not take condensation from the breath and will not form ice globules when the wearer exhales.

The bear was hunting for seal. The Eskimo was hunting for bear. Of the two, the big predator seemed the better able to survive; his great jaws held twin rows of gleaming fangs, his huge, rounded feet, with their thick pads of heavy hair, contained powerful claws. He measured over eight feet from the tip of his black nose to the end of his short tail and he was as strong as ten men and as agile as a cat. How could the small man with his puny spear inflict damage upon such a goliath?

Life for the bear and his sister began one dark morning in subzero January. Late during the previous June his mother had met a male on the edge of the tundra and the two had mated, stayed together briefly and then separated; like all bears, the white creature of the north travels alone, relying on no one for aid. The mother hunted as usual during the short summer of her second pregnancy and she grew fat from the eating of much meat. Then the summer ended and the nights became longer and the cold more biting, and at last, warned by some mysterious instinct, the she-bear went to look for a den.

In that region of flat barrens there is only one kind of territory that offers a female polar bear sanctuary from the cold: pressure ice—great slabs of thick ice that have been pushed upwards and lean in awkward disarray, like the walls and roof of some collapsed building. Here are crevices into which the bulging female may crawl, digging her way through a top layer of snow. Inside she may turn a few times, smoothing a place for her big body while the north wind is busy blowing snow back into the hole she has dug. Soon the hole is covered and the mother and her unborn young are snug for the winter.

When the twins arrived the sun had already disappeared behind the western horizon for the last time that year; it would not come again for many weeks and an almost perpetual darkness would continue outside the lair, making life hard for the males, old and young, and the females who had not become pregnant that season, for, unlike the grizzly and the black bears, only expectant polar bear mothers hibernate during the arctic freeze-up.

The cubs came into their cold world hairless and their tiny legs still needed time to become fully formed; their eyes were shut and each cub jostled with the other in its eagerness to snuggle into the warm fur of their 700-pound mother. They were minute beings, those two, each weighing less than two pounds and measuring only nine inches of scrawny length. Uncaring of all but the warm, milk-filled dugs of their mother, the little ones fed and slept and grew, warm in the fine fur that had grown about their bodies only five days after birth.

Slowly, week by week, the light outside the den grew stronger as the sun returned to change midnight into morning and the mother bear became restless in her sleep. One day, when a scant ray of sunshine brushed against the snowy doorway of her den, she opened her eyes and yawned, opening a cavernous mouth. She licked her son and daughter and whoofed at them gently before lumbering to her feet. In a moment her streamlined body burst through the snow and cold air rushed into the fetid ice cave; the cubs, undaunted by the frost, followed their mother. It was March, and a time

The polar bear is a master swimmer.

for hunting, and she led her cubs across the ice, searching the distance for the shape of a seal.

That afternoon she saw one. The hair seal rested only a few feet away from its blow-hole and all around flat ice would not allow the polar bear the chance to get close enough to strike. Then she searched the terrain; southeast of the seal a ridge of pressure ice offered concealment and the bear turned to it, the stubby cubs following at her heels, sensing the hunt already, inexperienced and young as they were. Behind the ice barrier the way to the choppy, ice-filled sea was clear. Then she stopped, looked at her cubs and grunted softly; it was an order, the first she had given them, but they knew its meaning. Each sank to the ice, curled its small body into a ball and watched the mother plod to the water's edge.

The bear entered the cold water with hardly a splash; her small, graceful head, long neck, and shapely body were built for this. For a moment her head was visible on the surface, then, taking a deep breath, she disappeared under the gray waves. Now she swam vigorously for the ice pack and the blow-hole, instinct guiding her at first, then, once she was under the ice, a faint reflection of light seeping downwards through the narrow hole. Moments later she was under it. It was too small for her to crawl through, but she reached up one huge forearm and scratched at the under-surface of the ice. In a flash the seal dived headfirst through the hole, straight into the arms of the great bear. It was dead in moments. The mother swam back to the ice-edge, holding her prey between her jaws. She climbed out some distance from the pressure ice but continued towards it, still dragging the seal, and soon she and her cubs feasted on the warm carcass.

Five years had passed since the day the bear was born. He was full grown, a monster who weighed three-quarters of a ton, and was just now getting ready to mate for the first time. Somewhere out on the ice, his twin sister, if she had survived, was experiencing the same mysterious urgings, for these ice creatures, unlike their cousins in the south, are slow to mature, perhaps in this way maintaining the balance of nature in this inhospitable land.

The female he chose that June day was old, probably mating for the last time, and not likely to give birth to more than one cub. The male found her riding on a large iceberg to which he had swum the night before during his incessant search for food. The two remained there for six days, eating of seal. Afterwards the male left, jumping into the water and heading out to sea, unafraid of venturing far into the ocean in his search for a new hunting ground. He swam almost twenty miles that day, swinging his specially jointed front legs in a wide circle. He was nearly tireless in the water and he kept going until a great mass of glaring ice loomed before him. He climbed on the berg's flank and rested awhile on the floating island, then he began looking around for food.

He lived well that summer and was in perfect condition when winter came, but now, trotting to outflank that which he thought was a seal, he was ravenously hungry. Earlier that day he had tried to stalk a seal; the fat ringed seal sat by its hole, unaware of the yellowish shape that was creeping towards it, snake-like neck extended, back legs trailing the body, its movements controlled by the powerful front legs which dragged the bear's great weight over the ice. But moments before he was ready to pounce on his prey, the ringed seal smelled him and in a flash was gone.

He was being more careful now, but again he was to be disappointed. Within half a mile of the dark patch he saw that this was an old hole; just a depression on the ice, sealed off from the water.

The short man in the heavy parka was crawling on his stomach, scuttling across the ice towards the big bear. About 500 yards from the predator he stopped, set aside his short spear, and rummaged in the bag he carried on his back. His naked hand came out holding a thin, six-inch piece of whalebone that was half an inch wide, its ends sharpened to fine points. The Eskimo put down the bone and thrust his hand deep into the recesses of his parka, producing a ball of whale fat about as big as his clenched hand. He had carried the fat next to his skin, keeping it from freezing this way. Now he kneaded it, giving it more roundness; he held the fat in his left hand and his right picked up the whalebone. Working swiftly he bent the bone into the shape of a U, keeping the pressure of his fingers upon it to prevent the tensile strip from springing back into its original shape; then he thrust the sharpened points deep into the fat, still maintaining pressure on the bone. He held the ball of fat in his mitted hand until the cold crept into it and froze it, trapping the bent bone inside.

The man crawled closer to the bear. When he was less than 200 yards from the great beast he lifted his right arm and

threw the ball of fat towards it. The ball was now frozen
hard. It rolled on its way, stopping only a short distance from
the bear. The Eskimo turned and began crawling away, back
to the safety of the ice ridge, and the bear, his keen nose always working, became suddenly aware of an odor that whet-
ted his hunger to greater intensity. He followed his nose and
soon found the fat. In one snap it was gone, swallowed
whole, and the bear sniffed about, seeking more of this mysterious food that had come to him so unexpectedly.

On the ridge the man watched the bear. The creature now
turned to the north, continuing his quest for food, not knowing that the warmth of his belly had been used by the man to
unleash a weapon that must surely kill him. Inside the bear's
maw the fat was slowly melting; the whalebone, still seeking
to return to its original shape, pushed against the softening
walls that held it captive. Soon the fat became soft and the
bone escaped. It shot out, a deadly, double-edged knife that
pierced the bear's bowels and made the great beast scream
with pain.

In the distance, following, came the small man. He would
follow for several days, as long as it took the bear to bleed to
death from the inside, then he would skin the massive beast
and take its claws and its teeth and perhaps some of its meat
and he would tramp the dreary, lonely miles back to his
home and his family, weighted by the heavy pelt.

Today it was the man's turn to live and the bear's to die.
Tomorrow, perhaps, some other bear would come and while
the small man was busy with another hunting quest the yellow-white giant would stalk him as though he were a seal and
the man would die.

Such is the way of the northland. It is a land of fear and
death, of hunger and of cold. It is a great land, a place that
shows man how to be humble, that teaches a great arctic bear
how to capture an elusive seal.

The Legend

He sat as though in sleep, humped back propped against a tree, legs stretched out on the pine needles that littered the ground, arms resting on a hairy paunch. The small eyes were merest slits as they peeked over the dishpan face, down the nose, away from the glare of the noon sun. Now and then a massive arm would move lazily and long yellow claws would scratch at the persistent itch on side or chest, otherwise he remained still, a grotesque brown shape enjoying a siesta midway up a mountain in the southern part of Alaska.

Occasionally the short ears flicked this way and that, routine listening that was in the nature of the beast, an uncaring alertness prompted by habit, but needless now, for he wasn't hungry or thirsty, and he was fearless.

He was a legend. An ugly, bad-tempered, hulking legend that had survived time and a thousand campfires that buzzed with the tales of his prowess. This was his domain, his own particular mountain, and all others that fearfully shared his habitat knew better than to disturb him while he sunned himself that summer morning.

He was fierce and powerful, a lordly grizzly bear male who had lived alone ever since he was weaned by his great mother eight summers ago. Yet he was not lonely. All the members of his species have lived solitary lives since time began; they are too quarrelsome for company, always ready for battle, and except for a brief mating period each year they wander where they will through their chosen domain, from the day when, as serious two-year-olds, they are chased into the world by their savage mothers.

This day the grizzly would doze late. He had killed that morning and he had gorged. Just before sun-up his nose had plucked the scent of elk from the mountain air and his ears had scooped up the faint noise made by the cloven hoofs. Using nose and ears, for his small, red-veined eyes were poor even in daylight, the big bear had stalked the small herd, optimistically, for he seldom got a chance to pull down one of the great deer of the Rockies. But this day had been different. There was among the band an old bull. His teeth, worn to crumbling ridges that barely rose over the gum line, had at last become useless to him; he was weak from hunger and made feeble by the parasites that infested his bowels and he lagged in the rear of the herd. Slowly the healthy band forged ahead along its browse line while the ancient one stumbled in the rear, stopping often for breath and grunting now and then from the pain that gnawed within his belly.

The grizzly found him during one of his stops. The bull, perhaps deaf, perhaps uncaring, remained still, his long neck hanging low and his broad head, mouth agape, angling along the ground, the black muzzle just inches from the rocky soil; his antlers, once symbols of regal prime, were merest spikes, misshapen gargoyles of bone that grew still but had not the nourishment to sustain the pride of their original form.

The grizzly came on, more than half a ton of hungry muscle, and the elk turned his neck. He saw the attacker moments before the huge paw flashed in the blow that broke his spine and thudded the old bull to the ground. The grizzly fed on the warm meat. He had killed quickly and well and the bull elk had found his release.

The bear woke late that afternoon and his empty stomach rumbled as he stretched his great body. He thought of the elk, but the grass of the meadow below was even more tempting than the meat, of which he had eaten an abundance early that morning. Flushing his nostrils with a big, grunting blow, he set out, lumbering down his trail, his broad rump with its short tail wagging almost comically, the pronounced hump over his shoulders rippling as his powerful chest and

"Silver tip" grizzly

leg muscles took the downhill strain. In the meadow he settled to his browse, pulling at the tender grasses. He browsed like an elk or a deer, packing green bulk into his huge stomach.

Habitually, the grizzly behaves rather similarly to his cousin, the black bear, but there are some important differences in his nature. He is considerably larger—an average grizzly will weigh 700 or 800 pounds, and some of the giants of the breed scale as much as three-quarters of a ton—fiercer and more belligerent, and grizzly sows make far better mothers than the black bears. The boars, especially the older, more crotchety males, are just as prone as the black bear males to devour their own offspring if they get the chance—which they seldom do, for the fierce mother is rarely far from her darling cubs until the youngsters are at least eighteen months old and able to take care of themselves.

Everybody has heard about the grizzly's great strength. The animal is, indeed, a legend in many countries of the world and though some of the prowess that has been ascribed to him is undoubtedly exaggerated, he is nevertheless enormously strong. He has been seen to carry loads that weigh almost a ton, and carry them long distances, too. With the exception of another grizzly, there is nothing that the hump-backed giant is afraid of, not even man, though he avoids him whenever possible. He will readily attack if he is provoked and many a rash hunter has been slashed to death by the mighty creature.

The grizzly bear is an animal of many deceptions. He looks slow, yet he can twist and turn at great speed and is agile enough to take spawning salmon from the creeks and rivers, something that I have tried to do many, many times and only achieved once, and then it was by accident! The grizzly also looks sleepily stupid, but this, too, is a pose. He is shortsighted, it is true, but his keen nose and ears are always on the alert, no matter how sleepy he looks.

Like the black bear, the grizzly enjoys the best of both worlds; in good weather he eats, sleeps, and roams about on his own, unconcerned, occasionally frisking exuberantly, now and then stopping at the foot of some great pine and reaching up, standing on his hind legs, to scratch at the sticky bark —travelers through the mountains often find these scarred trees, used again and again by one or more of the creatures.

The females, or sows as they are also called, mate every second or third year. As a rule two cubs are born; sometimes a young bear will give birth to a single cub and at other times sows have three and even four babies. The young are born during the mother's "twilight sleep", deep in some cave in the mountains in January, February or early March, about seven months after the mating. The cubs, like those of the black bear, are incredibly small at birth. The mother may weigh 700 pounds or more, but her babies barely tip the scales at half a pound. They grow slowly and take almost ten years to reach full maturity. Generally the mother takes care of them for eighteen months, but some mothers keep them until they are more than two years old.

The grizzly bear is not a fussy eater. When his big stomach craves food, anything will do. In the spring of the year, fresh from hibernation, the big bears feast on grass and shrubs and seek out carrion left by other predators. They dig up roots, ground squirrels, pikas and any other edible product of their habitat. About the only things safe from a grizzly grow or live in trees! Unlike his black cousin, the mountain bear can't climb, not more than a few feet from the ground anyway, a fact for which many a hunter can be thankful!

The grizzly's color varies considerably. Some are dark gray, going to black, others are brown, buff or pale yellow. A young grizzly, dark in color, has often been mistaken for a black bear, and in the far north light-colored grizzlies have even been taken for polar bears, though the two animals are physically unlike.

As a rule the grizzly is shy of man and likes nothing better than to avoid him. Often I have met grizzlies in the Rockies and on each occasion they have turned away and trotted off in the other direction, for which I was grateful. But while the great bear minds his own business most times, it is good practice to leave him strictly alone.

A few years ago I visited a hospital in Vancouver to interview two grizzly bear victims. Both men were lucky to be alive; one will carry the bear's teeth marks on his head for the rest of his life. The men and a companion were climbing in the Rockies when they startled a big male bear. Instead of leaving the big fellow alone they went closer to get some photographs and the grizzly charged them. He seized one by the head and shook him as a dog shakes a rat, then he dropped him and clawed the chest and shoulder of the second man; their companion ran to get help, but by the time the party arrived to the rescue the bear had gone, leaving his mauled victims where they had fallen.

Another grizzly might have stayed to make a meal of his victims, this one didn't. But that's typical of the grizzly; he's an unpredictable fellow.

Birth of a Miracle

He was blind, hairless and toothless, a pink, helpless thing that weighed a scant seven ounces when he wriggled from his sleeping mother one morning in January.

Through the thin eyelids that veiled his brown eyes came a soft light, the first impression of his new world to register in the virgin labyrinths of his brain. He didn't know it, but the light came diffused through a filter of snow that, could he have seen it, looked blue from the inside and was tinged on the outside by the yellow rankness of his mother's breath.

He was wet and cold, and this was another sensory awakening. Until the moment of his birth he had been gently cushioned within the warmth of his mother's womb.

He squealed. It was a thin noise that resembled in miniature treble the petulant hysteria of a hungry pig; because he didn't know what else to do, he continued uttering the wail. Still his mother slept and the cold congealed on his naked little body, crusting it with ice flakes that were made from the wetness of his birth, but instinct urged him towards the furred bulk of his mother. He wriggled to her on legs that were as yet hardly formed; his questing nose touched the edge of a big hind paw and he quickened his struggles.

His wailing ceased as a strange, urgent aroma assailed his nostrils and aroused awareness of the hunger that was within him. Soon he was encased within a muff of warm black fur and his eager mouth found and seized a full dug. He sucked greedily and some of the warm milk dribbled from between his black lips. After the feed he slept, his body stilled in the position it had adopted during the meal.

While he slept, grayness shrouded the snow skylight. Outside a blizzard ravaged the forest, swooping through the trees and shrubs in a crescendo of fury that mantled his yet unknown world with a cowl of white.

But the bear cub knew nothing of this. Inside the rock cave he and his great mother slept through the storm's wrath, secure on a warm bed of grasses and leaves and pine needles that succeeding generations of sleeping bears had deposited on the cave floor. This was a time of beginning for the cub, a time during which nothing was demanded of him except the will to live and to take sustenance from the fierce being that had given him birth during a fitful interruption of her winter sleep.

The cub ate, and he grew, and forty days later he felt an itching about his eyelids. He rubbed at the irritant with one paw and the gummy lids fluttered open.

Outside the cave a warming wind was attacking the snow and ice and preparing the land for its growing time. A full moon shed yellow light through the bush and some of it filtered through the naked arms of a tamarack that stood sentinel outside the cave.

The moonlight slanted through the now clearing ice barrier at the cave mouth and reached the cub, who blinked at it, then retreated fearfully into the folds of his mother's arms. Cautiously he peered from behind one of her thick paws, astounded at the suddenness of this new sensation, unaware of its source, but recognizing the power that it gave him. The small, dog-like head which was now covered in fine, black down thrust out and moved in slow semicircle, allowing the eyes to focus on the dimly-lit den.

The cub saw a small piece of tree branch. It was about the thickness of one of his forelegs and he moved towards it, driven by a growing discomfort inside his mouth. He closed his small jaws over the stick and began to bite it and the needle points of his new teeth pushed through the flesh of his gums. He growled his pleasure and began chewing ecstatically.

On that night the cub was twelve inches long and weighed two pounds; beside him, the bulk of his 200-pound mother loomed indistinctly in the semi-darkness, a warm mass that dwarfed to insignificance the diminutive being she had nurtured unknowingly. The she-bear was a young mother, for this was her first born. Later, when she reached breeding maturity and added perhaps another 100 pounds of weight to her bulk, she would give birth to two, three or even as many as four cubs—though two would most likely be her usual number.

The bear was three years old. Early last June she had mated for the first time, spending almost a month with the big, cinnamon-colored male, then leaving him as each set off on the solitary paths that are characteristic of the bear's independence from his kind. From that time on, until she became ready to mate again two years later, the sow would wander through the woods concerned only for herself and the cub she had produced.

Outside, it was spring. The mother bear rumbled to her feet and stretched the stiffness from her bones; she nuzzled the small cub, licking his head with her great tongue, grunting in affection. Then her eyes were drawn to the open cave-mouth and she stepped away from her baby and walked to the outside. When she stopped in the entrance to survey the area around her lair, the cub thrust his way between her back legs, taking refuge under her shaggy body from the immense newness that was before him. The mother turned her head and peered at the little face that showed shyly from under her ample skirt; she grunted and moved forward, leading the cub into the woods.

All that morning, while the cub frisked joyfully around her, the mother prowled about the area of her lair, stopping to nibble at cedar twigs or to chew at the early grass, her empty stomach rumbling and belching when she swallowed.

The mother was an untidy creature that day. The sleek coat in which she had bedded last winter was ragged and matted and already shedding many of its hairs, causing her body to itch. Much of her time that morning was spent rubbing against trees, scraping away the old hair and finding relief

from the irritation caused by the lost fur and the coming of her new coat; but she did not forget her cub.

The toddler, who weighed four pounds on that first morning, was learning the first of many lessons from his great mother. The she-bear was especially alert and frequently interrupted her tasks to stand man-like on her hind legs, sniffing for danger, peering shortsightedly with her small eyes for signs of enemies. Several times she fancied that threats were lurking in her area and she grunted at her cub; the youngster, obeying some urgency in her tone, immediately scrambled up the nearest tree, scaling it quickly despite his size, and edging his fat little body out along a branch that was just capable of carrying his weight. There he would stay, safe from heavier animals, whose bulk would not allow them to venture on the thin branch, until his mother, satisfied that there was nothing to fear, grunted her permission for him to come down.

Spring passed and gave way to summer and the cub grew strong and learned his lessons. He saw his mother turn over rocks, uncovering the ants and grubs that lay under them, and he found their taste agreeable to his palate; he watched her as she dug into the burrows of mice and groundhogs and captured the small creatures, which she shared with him. He learned to find carrion left by other predators and he learned how to tear open a rotten log, full of big carpenter ants that could be lapped up in thousands. He and his mother ate anything. Grasshoppers, birds and their eggs, shrubs, ferns, berries and roots and, for rare treats, honey from the wild bees, which wasted their stings on the shaggy coats and unfeeling faces of the two raiders. And then autumn came.

The cub weighed over forty pounds and he and his mother became busy feeding and storing fat on their bodies for the long sleep that lay ahead.

One day, when the maples stood naked and their red leaves lay dying on the forest floor, the first snow fell; big, slow flakes that drifted down and settled. Soon the woods became clouded with the falling white and the trees and

---

Black bear cub with an itch

bushes and the earth were covered by the crystals. The she-bear sought a lair.

The old cave was forgotten and too far to reach and the mother searched for two days before she found what she was looking for. The new den was inside a giant pine, a rotten, ancient tree which lay on the forest floor, hollowed by insects and the weather and animals, and which offered sanctuary to the she-bear and her cub.

They went to sleep, but it was not the death-like slumber of true hibernation. The temperature of their bodies did not fall and though their breathing slowed, they filled their lungs with air five or six times every minute; if they were disturbed they would wake and if their den was not comfortable they would leave it and seek new quarters elsewhere. They did not eat, because there was no need. The layers of fat which they stored on their bodies during summer and autumn nourished them and made it unnecessary for them to leave their warm lair to seek food and water.

The cub was happy. Sleep was with him and there was spring to look forward to.

But there was a time of sadness ahead. It would come next June, when the cub would be almost two years old. His mother was to suddenly ignore him and a gruff male bear was to threaten him and he was to be driven from them.

He would den alone that winter, sheltering under some snow-covered deadfall, while his mother, asleep and unaware, gave life to her new cubs.

Old Coon's Tale

The raccoon's Latin name, *lotor,* means "the washer", and for as long as anyone can remember this masked, ring-tailed mammal has been credited with washing his food before eating it. The fact of the matter is, though, he does no such thing!

How, then, did this animal acquire a reputation that has been echoed in the writings of naturalists for so many years? The myth must have begun with the first white settlers to arrive on this continent, who observed the raccoon wading in streams and at the edges of lakes and beaver ponds, hunting for some of its food. They must have noted the animal's sensitive hands constantly on the go, feeling for prey, catching frog or minnow or clam and eating it. Later, perhaps, somebody captured a young raccoon and kept it as a pet and fed it, so that it had no need to hunt, and that, I believe, is where the "washing" idea really began.

Deprived of its need to hunt—a need that generations of wilderness survival had impressed deeply into the raccoon's instincts—captive coons who were assured of an easy and continuous supply of food still could not deny this urge. As a result, they carried their food to the water dish and dunked it, "losing" it and then capturing it again, going through an age-old ritual that observers mistook for a fastidious habit.

Years ago, when I first became acquainted with raccoons, I readily accepted their supposed washing habits, but I wondered why they did it, why they had become the only animals apart from man that felt the need to wash their food. I searched the record. One explanation, still accepted by some people today, was that raccoons have either poor salivary glands or none at all. It seemed reasonable to me at the time. Another theory was that they derive pleasure from feeling the food under water with fingers that are extremely sensitive. This, too, appeared to make sense. I let matters go at that and clung to these false trails for a long time, despite the fact that of the first fourteen raccoons that I studied in the wild, only one showed any interest in dunking his food in water before eating it and, significantly, that one had been raised as a pet by city people and kept in a cage until he became too much of a nuisance. His owners then asked me if I would take him and keep him on my wilderness property. I did, and because he was old enough to survive on his own in the forest, I released him.

At the time I used to keep a feeding platform against the kitchen window of my log house, and all manner of wild animals would come to it, raccoons included. Often I would sit in my kitchen with the lights out and watch as relays of raccoons came to eat the leftovers and other foods that I had put out. Having regard for their washing habits, I had gone to a good deal of trouble to fix a round, galvanized basin at one end of the feeder, and for some time it worried me that my wild raccoons did not appear to like this bath. They never took the food to it and washed it! Yet they did go and drink from it when they were thirsty. I tried various ways of making this tub of water more attractive to my visitors, but in vain.

Then the pet raccoon came to call. Sure enough, he took all his food to the tub, balanced on the edge, and dunked away for several seconds before putting the food in his mouth. This set me to thinking.

By this time I had raised a number of orphan coons until they were old enough to fend for themselves, but I had not kept any of them in a cage, allowing them instead the freedom of a special room that I had built within a shed, where the animals could roam around and do some hunting for insects and the occasional mouse. After they were released they quickly found the feeder, and on occasion two or three of them would show up (day or night, for raccoons are not to-

Raccoon

tally nocturnal) and take peanuts from my hand, or marshmallows, and perch on my lap while they dined.

Often they would come right into the kitchen, sit on the counter, and accept whatever I had for them—but no washing! Feeling, yes; that was another story. As a rule, while they were eating a peanut or some other tidbit, their hands would be poking and feeling continuously, sometimes at my clothing, other times at my own hands. Often they would stick their hands into kitchen utensils. Those hands were almost constantly on the move. But, such was my obtuseness, I did not begin to understand until after some twenty-six wild raccoons had put their trust in me and my feeder to the point where I could sit and watch them as they fed.

Finally, those raccoons made me realize that *lotor* does not wash his food. Only that one, the pet, had shown any interest in the washtub. After this I spent many weeks on the shores of lakes and beaver ponds, seeking raccoons and watching them as they hunted, studying them by day, and by night when the moon was bright enough, through field glasses. Over a period that extended from mid-May until early September I observed no less than forty-nine raccoons hunting and eating in the wild. Not one of them washed its food! Often some of them appeared to be washing, but they were in fact selecting, making sure that what they had fished out of the water was edible and tossing away anything that was not, such as empty clamshells, pieces of waterlogged bark, or stones.

As to the idea that raccoons have poor salivary glands, this is patent nonsense. I have often had my fingers in their mouths and watched as they masticated dry foods such as bread, and I can certify that they have quite sufficient saliva for their eating needs.

I wrote about these findings in a newspaper article some years ago and was gratified, about two months later, to see confirmation of my theory by Desmond Morris, the noted British biologist and author of *The Naked Ape.* Dr. Morris wrote in the now defunct *Life* magazine about the effects of close confinement on animals in zoos and illustrated his points with, among other animals, the raccoon, pointing out that in his view the myth about raccoons and food washing was based on observation of animals whose habits had been changed by captivity.

Raccoons, which range across most of the United States and southern Canada, are cousins to the bear and, like him, they eat anything, often! This means *anything,* animal or vegetable, fresh or stale, raw or cooked, sweet or savory—just name it and raccoons will eat it. From spring, when they come out of their dens, to late autumn, when they seek sleep (they do not hibernate in the strict sense of the word), eating, or looking for food, occupies about sixty-five per cent of their time.

They appear to prefer foraging from early evening to about one or two o'clock in the morning, but they frequently hunt and fish in broad daylight. It just depends on how well they have fed the night before and whether or not they have found a comfortable enough perch on which to sleep off the effects of their last meal.

Mating takes place in January or February, depending on location, earlier matings being the rule in warmer climates. In the northern limits of their range, where raccoons den up in a hollow tree or an underground burrow to sleep through the cold weather, they emerge in February for a short courtship; then, if the weather is still cold, they go back to their dens until spring sunshine calls them outside once more.

Nine weeks after the mating, from two to six young ones are born, fully furred and already sporting the family mask and the ringed tail, though their eyes are still closed. Twenty days later the young coons begin to leave the den with their mother on short trips. By three months of age they are about half the size of the mother and follow her wherever she wanders, by this time already feeling her anger when competition over food takes place. Soon after that, the mother goes off on hunting trips of her own, leaving the young to forage for themselves, though she generally returns to them at bedtime.

The family usually den up together that autumn. In February the young females emerge with their mother and mate for the first time; but though the young males may wake up at this time also, they do not usually breed until they are two years old. This difference in breeding maturity between the sexes in a litter is, I believe, nature's way of cutting down on inbreeding, thus keeping the species healthy.

Coon Cousins

It was late August, a dry-hot afternoon. I had been sitting quietly on a rock watching three bob-white quail dining on sweet gum seeds. This was to be my last day in Texas, where I had spent three weeks seeking animals and birds native to the south. I had been fortunate in finding and studying a number of these during my camping trip, but the one animal that I had especially wanted to observe had eluded me until then. Ringtails, I had been told, are shy creatures and not easy to find and they do most of their traveling and hunting at night. At that point, I could confirm these statements.

The quail had arrived about five minutes after I had settled myself on the rock; they were unaware of my presence and I was endeavoring to keep still so as not to startle them. Suddenly the birds scooted away into the underbrush, making their strange little cries. I wondered what had alarmed them and was about to get up when I heard an explosive bark coming from about midway up the tall sweet gum under which I was sitting. I looked up.

At first I could see nothing but the star-shaped leaves of the sweet-smelling tree. Then I noticed movement, and in another moment there was an inquisitive, friendly little face peering down at me. I had found my ringtail—or it had found me!

The big, soft eyes surrounded by their white circles continued to watch me, apparently quite unconcerned by my presence, though the sharp, almost fox-like muzzle with its sensitive nose seemed to be taking in my scent. The visitor made no more barking noises, but continued to stare.

Ringtail, or cacomixtle

When I travel in search of wild animals I generally carry a variety of tidbits about my person to tempt the more daring to come closer. On this occasion, peanuts in the shell occupied one of my pockets, and in the other was a partly-filled plastic bag of marshmallows. I had been told that ringtails have a sweet tooth, so I decided to try my luck. Moving slowly so as not to frighten the stranger, I fished out three marshmallows and held them up, letting him catch their scent. Almost immediately the ringtail's long nose began moving furiously. I waited for perhaps two minutes, then the animal moved forward. Now I could see all of its fifteen-inch, buff-colored body and its long, bushy black-banded tail.

With my thumb I flicked a marshmallow and it landed beyond the tree, about thirty feet from where I was sitting. The ringtail's keen eyes watched it in flight and the nose worked some more. Soon the animal slithered around the tree, where I couldn't see it, and I heard it slide down. Silence for about three more minutes. At last the curious, pleasant face poked out from behind the tree, looked at me, and withdrew; then its owner appeared in a rush, grabbed the marshmallow and slithered back up the tree.

There, about fifteen feet from the ground but in full view, it devoured this delicious new food. When it was finished I threw another marshmallow. After the fourth sweetmeat, the ringtail didn't bother to go back up the tree; it just sat where the food landed and ate it, watching me all the time. In all, I threw seven marshmallows and the ringtail showed absolutely no sign of fear. When it was finished eating it sat on its hind legs and washed its paws and face, and it only scampered up the tree when I rose to go.

Once more I was reminded that no naturalist should allow himself to accept generalizations about any species. Again and again I had expected a particular animal to be shy and fearful, only to find that it responded quite readily to a quiet approach and, sometimes, to softly-spoken words. The fact is, of course, that animals, like people, are individuals.

Ringtails range from South and Central America up to southwestern Oregon and western Colorado, preferring areas of rocky outcroppings, scattered pines, and clear running water.

The young are born in shallow caves or inside dead trees in May or early June. There are four or five in a litter and they are about the size of domestic kittens. The mother apparently takes most of the responsibility for raising them, though some naturalists report that the male helps with the task at times.

At first the little ringtails are blind and toothless and their ears are closed. Their pink bodies have a meager coating of whitish hair, and the dark rings are already visible on their tails. The first sound they make is a squeak, like the protest of a rusty hinge; they emit that noise when they are hungry, which is often!

By the time they are three weeks old their mother's milk is no longer sufficient for their eager appetites, and when she leaves the den to hunt she returns with meat for the kits. In another six weeks they travel with one or both parents on hunting trips, and at four months the babies are pushed out into the world, on their own. By now their squeak has turned to a short, spitting bark whenever they are angry or afraid.

The ringtail will eat almost anything. Though its favorite food is meat, it also enjoys such side dishes as fruit, nuts, vegetables, insects, and the local farmer's corn. Despite the little damage that it does to cultivated crops, this relative of the raccoon is a valuable ally in keeping down mice, rats, and other vermin, for it is an able hunter and catlike in its ability to pounce on its prey.

Long before the coming of the white man, the Aztecs had a name for the ringtail, *cacomixtle,* and this is how it is still known south of the United States border.

The coatimundi, which is sometimes mistaken for either the raccoon or the ringtail, is, if only by appearance, a clownish creature that likes to run in bands (except the male, who prefers his own company). To my way of thinking, it looks like a badly-drawn raccoon, a sort of cartoon coon with an exaggerated tail that most times it carries poker-straight.

In fact, the first time I saw a band of female coatis and their young, the thing that initially caught my attention was their tails, a strange sight as these black and white ringed appendages moved above the top of a large clump of bushes. I was watching from a distance with field glasses, so the animals were unaware of my presence when they emerged into full view. The band was foraging, a thing they do well and which seems to occupy all their time for they are as omnivorous as raccoons, to which species they are related. They hunt for small rodents, birds' eggs, fruit, insects, and carrion.

I knew that coatis are agile, but I did not realize just how quick and monkey-like they really are until, wanting to get a better look at them, I rose from a crouch and began walking slowly towards them. Immediately the band exploded for the shelter of a convenient tree, hissing and spitting and waving their long tails in excitement.

Apart from a short courtship period, the male coati lives

alone. The females have their young in September or October, about eleven weeks after mating, when from three to five babies are born in a tree-den, a cave, or an abandoned burrow. They develop rapidly and before long are trotting around with their mothers and learning to be independent.

Coatis are common in Central and South America and less so, though numerous enough, in southwestern New Mexico and southern Arizona. Although this species is thoroughly at home in the trees, its members spend a considerable time on the ground as well, where, alert and agile though they are, they face danger from the larger meat eaters.

The coati is a slender animal with an elongated head and a long, flexible snout that protrudes beyond its lower jaw. Its canine teeth are like miniature knives and are capable of inflicting serious wounds. A big male will measure between four and five feet in length, including tail, and weigh up to twenty pounds; the female is little more than half this size.

The color of its coat varies from one individual to another; it may be grizzled brown, gray, or black and yellow with shadings of white on the chin and throat. And it is the big white nose, the white-circled eyes and the extremely long barred tail that give the coatimundi the clownish appearance already referred to.

Coatimundi

Treetop Marauders

She is lying on the branch of a leaning pine, a large, golden-brown bundle of energy with a bushy, fox-like tail, rounded ears set well back on her head and the face of an elf. Her mouth is open, disclosing a pink tongue and rosy gums and a set of sharp, gleaming teeth. Now she is at rest, satisfied after a successful hunt, and the forest is at peace again, for the tree-top marauder is not flashing from pine to spruce in chase of a chattering, terrified squirrel.

It is a savage creature, this pine marten, and it is hostile to all things, including its own kind. Yet, and despite the efficiency with which it kills, it is an attractive, likable creature, all fangs and fury to the animals of its world, full of impudent curiosity towards man, who seems to be the only exception on its hate list. And this is irony, for man is its greatest enemy! It is a meat eater, and one of the fastest harriers of the forest, but it does not waste and it does not kill just for the pleasure of it, as some of the predators do.

Perhaps its greatest fondness is for the red squirrel, a small, agile creature that to a human seems to move with the quickness of sound; but compared to the marten, the little red squirrel is a doddering cripple! It is really a case of anything the squirrel can do, the marten can do better. It can flash through the most slender tree-tops, outjump the squirrel, and seldom lose its balance. Unless the squirrel can find safety in a tree hole too small for the marten to enter, it is lost.

Lying on the tree limb, the marten does not look very

Pine marten

fierce or very fast; seen by a man, she is like a strange mixture of dog and cat, a grinning, cuddly animal that seems to invite friendship. In reality the creature is one of the wildest in the forest and shuns populated places.

This is an easy time for the marten. It is middle June and mating time is still a month away, so the female in the tree is at peace with herself; her last year's brood have grown up and left their dark cavity in a hollow poplar, and the female has only one thing to worry about—food. Because she is a good hunter this is a small problem, for there are many red squirrels in this part of the wilderness and the region is far enough away from the haunts of man to ensure her protection. Of course there are those she fears, such as the fisher, which is even faster than the marten; and the great golden eagle, if she is careless enough to get caught out in the open, which she rarely is; and then there is the lynx, the silent hunter that may be her most dangerous enemy.

In another part of the backwoods a big, dark creature, similar to the marten but for its larger size, is sleeping in a den under some rocks. This is the fisher, an animal about the size of a fox and one of the fastest creatures of the wilderness; if the marten can outrun the squirrel, the fisher can outrun the marten, and since it is bigger and stronger it has little trouble killing its distant relative.

Both animals belong to the weasel family and both have musk glands that can be unpleasantly odorous when they are aroused, but there is little else in common between the two, unless it be a bad temper. The fisher's long, bushy tail signals its moods of anger; it starts by twitching when the animal is displeased and accelerates its side-to-side motion when its owner becomes really angry; then the fisher arches its back, looking rather like another relative, the wolverine, and charges its enemy or its prey.

The fisher has one distinction which few other meat-eating animals have: it can attack and kill a porcupine with impunity, for it is so fast that it collects relatively few barbs. One flash of its jaw or paw and the porcupine is flipped on its back and

Fisher

the fisher attacks the soft, unprotected belly. In a trice the porcupine is dead and the giant weasel settles to its meal. Somehow, when quills do penetrate the fisher's skin, they rarely go deeper, but are turned before they pierce the muscle layer and work their way out again without causing the terrible, festering sores that are their trade mark on other creatures. Occasionally quills do get through and enter the digestive tract, but, mysteriously, they often go right through without hurting the fisher. Now and then a quill does take effect and the hunter dies—but rarely.

The fisher asleep in the rock den is a male. Somewhere in the forest there is a female who is raising a brood of young ones and has already mated for the second time. Just after her three kits were born she rushed out, looking for a new mate. Gestation time for these animals is long, between eleven months and a year, because the development of the fertilized eggs does not begin until the following spring. This is why the creature seeks a new mate immediately after having her

139

young, otherwise she could have young only every second year.

Young fishers are born blind and stay that way for seven weeks; they are naked and grow slowly at first, not being ready to go out hunting with mother until they are about three months old; from then on, they grow quickly and by the next autumn they leave home and go out to fend for themselves.

In winter fishers remain active; they don't like the bad storms and usually wait them out in their dens, but as soon as the snow stops falling, out they come, hungry and furiously seeking something to eat. They have to be more careful now, for the deep snow slows their bounding pace and they must travel at a walk.

While it is an interesting creature, the fisher is not as endearing as the marten, though its musk smell is not as fierce. Since its coat is valuable, it is much sought by trappers, and perhaps this is why few fishers are seen near civilization. But the animal has a temper equal to if not surpassing that of the marten! When angry it growls, snarls and hisses and arches its back at the foe. Sometimes it will stamp its forefeet against a tree-trunk, trying to scare the enemy with noise, for it is a bit of a coward. If it can avoid a fight it will, but if pressed into a corner, it becomes a fury and can come out the victor in an encounter with dog or fox or coyote. It weighs an average of twelve pounds but has been known to reach almost twenty, and with its speed, long fangs and agility, it can be a dangerous opponent.

The marten, too, takes its time about having babies, not quite as long as the fisher, but for the same reason. It does not rush out to seek a mate just after the babies are born. It raises the young ones first; then, any time between mid-July and the first three weeks of August, it mates. From one to five young ones are born the following April in a hollow log nursery, or, rarely, in a burrow underground. The little ones are covered in very fine, brownish hair and they stay blind for the first six weeks of their life.

Martens grow up quickly. In three months they are as big as their mother and weigh about two pounds, though some of the males may put on another pound or so by the time they reach adulthood. In autumn they leave home and start hunting alone, but by then they can look after themselves and don't go hungry too often. Now and then they meet each other and usually mind their own business, not looking for the company of their relatives, but sometimes they quarrel and then they growl and snarl and hiss, making almost more noise than an angry wolverine—but not quite!

Martens have an unusual way of marking the paths that they travel; in addition to the two anal musk glands, they also have a third gland in the center of their stomach, between the skin and the muscle wall. This gland is about three inches long and one inch wide and there are two openings in the belly skin beside it. When the marten walks along, over rocks and logs and up trees, it can, if it wants to, leave its calling card, discharging some of this musk, leaving a clearly-marked trail for other martens to follow.

The woods are deep in the shadows of evening now and the marten is sitting upright on the pine limb, looking rather like a small dog. Again she is hungry, but the squirrels have gone to sleep and the marten knows she cannot expect her favorite meal tonight. But she is not a fussy eater; rabbits, hares, shrews, mice, birds or their eggs, frogs (if she can catch them without getting wet, for all martens hate water), insects, carrion and even fruits and nuts, all these will do when she is hungry.

The sun is no more than a faint suggestion of pink far beyond the tree-tops when the female marten begins to move; she climbs the pine, moving easily along the swaying branches, and she jumps into another tree. For perhaps half an hour she travels this way, going from tree to tree, stopping often to smell at the dusk and to listen for the sound of running life beneath, then she comes to an open space. Down the tree she runs, headfirst, until she reaches the ground. She stops again, remaining motionless for almost fifteen seconds, listening to the sounds of a mouse scurrying through the grass. In a flash the marten locates the mouse and moves like a blur, pouncing on it before the small brown creature can utter so much as a squeak. Quickly, the mouse is swallowed and the marten licks her lips before going on, still hungry and looking for more food.

Walking at his clumsy weasel trot the fisher is approaching the marten's territory; both animals must meet if they continue their course, but neither is yet aware of the other's presence. The fisher, too, is hungry; he has not eaten all day and is hunting with more stealth than the marten for he has greater need. Moving among the ferns and small bushes that cover the forest floor the fisher is almost invisible, so well does his dark, silky hair blend with the land; his pace may look clumsy, but the big weasel is covering about four feet each time he jumps, each leap taking him closer to the marten.

Now the fisher is only twenty yards from the clearing in which the marten has killed the mouse; he stops, hearing the stealthy movements of the other hunter. At first the fisher is not sure. He must know what kind of creature is out there in the darkness. Crouching behind a dead balsam fir, the fisher waits, his small ears straining to the sound, his slightly upturned nose testing the breeze. He sits up, alert and interested, for he has smelled marten and hunger rumbles pleasantly in his capacious stomach.

The fisher moves slowly to the edge of the clearing, keeping low against the ground. It is quite dark now, but if the hunter cannot see, he can hear and smell and he knows that the marten is close. Soon the keen eyes detect slight movement on the ground about ten feet away and the fisher uncoils his taut body and dashes at the quarry.

Taken by surprise, the marten lets out one terrified squeal and races for the trees. The two predators are now moving so fast that it would be almost impossible to see them. This may be a race to the death, a spectacular race, for the runners are the two fleetest hunters of the wilderness!

The marten is already in a pine tree and she flashes through it, jumping fifteen feet into a spruce. In another moment the fisher is taking the same leap, but the marten is already three trees away. Faster yet moves the fisher and now he begins to overtake the desperate marten, who redoubles her efforts. The forest is silent, seeming to be waiting breathless for the outcome of this strange tree-top race.

It looks as though the marten is doomed. But no! This is her territory and she knows that near here there is a jumble of granite rocks and under them there is a den, a narrow, twisting tunnel leading to a chamber just large enough for the supple marten. If she can reach this she will be safe, for the big fisher will not be able to follow her. Faster still she streaks through the trees, the quicksilver, tireless fisher hot on her heels; now there are only a few yards to go and if the marten can just manage to keep ahead a little longer she will live this night. Almost at the point of exhaustion, she scrambles down the last tree and streaks across four feet of rough ground to the entrance of the rock den; in another moment she is gone and the furious claws of the fisher rake the place where seconds earlier her warm brown body had been. The fisher tries to follow, but the rock tunnel is too narrow, and presently the big hunter gives up, going in search of easier prey.

Inside the den the marten is spent; she lies curled up, her pink mouth agape, her red tongue lolling out, jerking with each sharp intake of her breath. She is still hungry, but she will not eat tonight; her fear will keep her in this place until morning. But hunger is a thing that can be endured if death is to be the price of a full belly.

The Brown Savage

The small beaver lake huddles in a granite cup surrounded by great dark rocks and overlooked by poplars and pines; along the banks, tenaciously clinging to scant soil, willows and alders fight for space. Moss grows on the rocks nearest the water and cattails have found footing in shallow recesses of waterlogged mud that creep away from the lake. In the water there is an army of dead trees; they stand erect, poplars and pines and birches, their bark long gone, their trunks punctured by the sharp bills of woodpeckers, their tops broken and ragged. On the surface of the water is a vast carpet of broad, shiny-green leaves punctuated now and then with yellow and white wax-like flowers resembling squat tulips; leading down from the leaves are slimy, ropelike stems that plunge into the turgid depth and end in the tuberous roots of the water lily, favorite food for beaver and muskrat.

The sun is high; the air is clear; birds are busy over the water. Swallows swoop back and forth, their great mouths open as they scoop minute insects out of the air; red-winged blackbirds chant their praises of a late spring as they flit from tree to bush, showing the splashes of red on their shoulders. Their nests are in the dead trees, perhaps on top, in a cuplike depression of the ragged crown, or a large woodpecker hole may serve instead.

The lake appears peaceful, as though in slumber; in the shallows a school of minnows feed on invisible organisms, while above the sound of the birds and the soft cooing of the breeze the steady splash of the dam drones on, a chant that even in midwinter never really stills.

Leading into the lake, on its south shore, a fast creek sprawls into a wide swirl as it enters the bigger water; up-creek, on both sides of the bank, just under the surface, muskrat tunnels show that the big rodents are plentiful here, but despite the quiet of the day none of the rats are visible. And this is not strange, for swift, merciless death has come to visit them and they cower in their underground chambers, hoping that the hunting mink will pass them by.

There goes the killer, on the far bank, a dark brown, two-foot, streamlined creature with a splash of white on his chest; he stands on a rock at the water's edge, his chocolate-brown fur dripping moisture.

The mink is not yet hungry enough to tackle a muskrat in its den; the rats are vicious fighters and have courage, and though the mink can kill them, he is likely to take more than one nasty bite before his victim stiffens in the agony of death. That is why the brown male has been scouting the water, swimming agilely under the surface, seeking the telltale muddy disturbance left by a fleeing muskrat. The mink hopes to find a rat returning from its feeding grounds and if he does, the battle will be short, for the killer can quickly dispose of a rat caught in the open. A rush or two, a couple of fast twists and the curved canine fangs of the mink pierce the muskrat at the base of its small brain.

Standing on the rock, the mink holds his forelegs stiff and his hindlegs are partly bent, raising the shoulders and showing the long, supple neck that tapers to a pointed, inquisitive face. The creature's short, rounded ears are set close to his head, the tip of his nose moves slightly as it probes the breeze, and his black eyes scan the water for signs of movement. The mink moves. Now he ambles at a slow pace, head down, bushy tail trailing, back arched. This is the mink's normal walk; he can, when chasing prey, break into a fast, bounding run which quickly brings him level with the creature that he is chasing, but he is too careful a hunter to hurry when he is searching for a meal.

The mink moves along the creek, scanning the water, but taking time now and then to look toward the bushes that line the shore, for lingering under these coverts there might be a

Mink

mouse or two, or a rabbit. Suddenly he stops. A slight riffle on the surface of the flowing creek has attracted his keen eyes; an indistinct shape is moving slowly, hugging bottom, just ahead of the riffle; it is a muskrat, aware by the absence of its neighbors that danger is near, but still some way from the safety of its bank den. The rodent moves cautiously, keeping close to the bottom, but this is a mistake, for its paddling, webbed feet stir up sand and debris which the current grasps and lifts higher, showing the mink where his prey is swimming. In an instant the sleek figure of the killer cleaves the surface water as he dives, a fast, free-moving interceptor now.

The muskrat hears him. Frantic, it pushes closer to the bottom and deliberately stirs up the sand, trying to provide a screen for itself; the mink advances, overtaking the slow rat, guided by its movements rather than by the sight of its body. In a moment the mink is alongside the fleeing rat; a quick lunge and the rapier teeth find their mark. The rat shudders once and is dead and the mink grips its body with his mouth and swims to the surface. Another predator would eat its kill on the bank, or at best drag it a little distance from the creek to a place of concealment; not the mink. These creatures prefer to take their food home and eat it in the comfort of their dens. So the two-pound mink emerges from the water with the body of the three-pound rat; effortlessly he shambles away, holding his head high to counterbalance the weight of his kill, and he does not stop until he has reached the privacy of his den, a roomy chamber inside the trunk of a fallen pine.

The mink is alone this year. He mated several times during March and finally settled down with a small female, setting up their quarters in the downed pine. If all had gone well the female would have given birth to four or five kits about fifty-two days later, but three weeks after the mating a trap forgotten by a careless trapper snapped shut about her head. She died quickly, and the male was left alone. It was too late to find another mate, so he remained in his bachelor quarters, hunting and prowling through his territory, always looking for a kill.

He may have felt lonely, but this is doubtful; animals don't "feel" as humans do, though vague recollections of other years may have coursed through his primitive brain, occasionally causing a restlessness to run through his sleek body, for now was the time of the young and other mink in the forest were busy caring for their broods. During past years at this time he had hunted for his mate and for the young kittens that mewed feebly in the den and he had been kept busy through the spring and summer, helping the female take care of the babies.

There is mystery surrounding the birth of mink young. At best it can be said that mink mothers take fifty-two days, on the average, from mating to birth time, but this can vary from forty-two to as many as seventy-five days, due to the arrest of the embryo inside the mother's womb; what causes this cessation of growth is not yet known. Mink mothers almost invariably give birth to their young between late April and mid-May, regardless of the time of mating, and this is another mystery, for it seems that some hidden impulse prompts some females to breed early, often in mid-February, while others will not accept a male until early or mid-March. And yet a third puzzle remains; most mammal females increase their food intake during late pregnancy and especially after their young are born, but mink mothers seem to go off their feed, consuming only about two-thirds of their normal ration, and they continue this habit until the kits start to eat solid food.

On an average four to five young are in a litter; but some females may have as many as seven or eight. The little ones are about as long as a human thumb and they are covered by fine, whitish hair at birth. They are blind until they are about five weeks old and they have a plaintive, cat-like mew. They are pretty, roly-poly little things. Even before their eyes open they exhibit their carnivorous appetites and chew at bits of meat brought to them by their mother and father; when they are able to see, they live entirely on a meat diet. If it is necessary to move the young, either the male or the female picks them up by the scruff of the neck when they are on land; in the water the little ones ride on their parents' backs. They are savage little beings, and when they play, which is often, their nature shows in their games and it is easy to imagine them three months later as they slink in for the kill.

As soon as they are strong enough to travel, the kits follow mother and father on hunting trips and they learn quickly how to stalk and slash. Now, older and more independent, they quarrel violently among themselves, hissing and growling and spitting at each other, already showing the unsociable characteristics that keep these ruthless hunters alone for more than half of every year; but perhaps their quarrelsome nature helps them later to become efficient at killing, which they must do well if they are to survive in the hard school into which they are born. From their parents they inherit the savagery of their kind and learn the ways of the wilderness; they are taught to hunt on land and most of all they are taught how to hunt in the water, for a mink is never far away from a stream, a river or a lake, where it can find fish or muskrats or waterfowl.

Quickly the kits adapt to the hard life of the predator. They become graceful, agile swimmers and learn to take fish easily; slowly they graduate to larger kills and by late summer, just before the family breaks up, each mink going its own way to lay claim to its hunting preserves, the young are capable of killing any of the fish, fowl or mammals that provide them with life.

When autumn comes the mink becomes solitary. Males wander through a larger range than females, hunting over a radius of one square mile or more; the females stay within an area of twenty or thirty acres; and each avoids the other.

Winter provides no great danger for mink, unless they live in a territory that is trapped by man; few animals care to tackle these fierce brown creatures, though the lynx and the bobcat and the fox will kill them. From the sky comes another danger. The snowy owl and the great horned owl will kill mink. Swooping down during the winter night, these great birds have little difficulty picking out the dark mink against the snow, for the mink's coat does not change to white in winter.

Even so, the mink is a formidable adversary. It can dodge in a flash and find shelter in the blink of an eye. In a corner it fights fiercely, hissing and spitting and showing its shiny, needle-like fangs and the sharp, curved claws on its forefeet. And it has another defense; it is a musk carrier and has twin glands like the skunk, though it cannot spray its stench. The smell is harsh, perhaps more unpleasant than the discharge of the skunk, and when a mink is angry or frightened it contracts its anal glands and discharges some of its obnoxious fluid.

Matilda

Matilda was a skunk. She was black, with the characteristic white stripes which ran from the base of her bushy tail, along her flanks and joined together at her head before continuing as one thinner line right to the tip of her shiny, inquisitive nose. I met her at two o'clock one summer morning, while I was camping alone in the Ontario backwoods, and I almost shot her. At first she was saved because she was too close to me and, had I murdered her, she would have repaid me by stinking out my tent and entire campsite with the evil liquid which these pretty little animals are so quick to spray at their enemies. As it was, on first acquaintance, when she was crawling into my tent, under the zipper, all I could think of doing for the protection of myself and my belongings was to squirt her first with one of those pressurized cans of insect spray I happened to have beside me.

Her head and shoulders were already in the tent and the beam of my flashlight, illuminating her, didn't bother her at all; but the insect spray did. Probably she was astounded that the creature whose lair she was invading was also capable of spraying its enemies with a liquid which, if not as lasting or evil smelling as her own, at least held an unpleasant enough odor and was extremely cold on contact with the skin. At any rate, Matilda's head and shoulders were quickly withdrawn from my tent and I was able to crawl out of my sleeping bag with some semblance of dignity and, instead of leaving the tent by cutting my way through its wall, as I would almost certainly have done had she succeeded in invading my canvas shelter, I made a normal, though cautious, exit through the front entrance.

I supposed that having been shown by the campsite occupant that she was not welcome there that night, Matilda would take the hint and leave quietly for other parts, but she obviously had no intention of leaving me that night. Foolishly, I had neglected to wash the frying pan in which I had fried my supper bacon and Matilda had found this by the time I emerged from the tent. When I located her with my light she was busy lapping up the bacon fat from the pan and though I shouted, stamped my feet and made as though to advance on her in what I hoped was a threatening manner, she refused to be intimidated.

At this point I was still prepared to execute her, but she was too close, and finally, checkmated by her at every turn, I gave up and decided to watch her. To do this better, and also with a hope, albeit a faint one, that she just might leave if more light was available, I primed my gasoline lantern and lit it. When the strong white light flooded the campsite Matilda looked up at me and, I'm positive, actually smiled approval. Now she could see as well as smell and since she had finished the bacon fat, she left the pan and started looking around, seeking other discarded tidbits, and she walked directly towards me.

Discretion told me to retreat and let Matilda have the campsite, but by then I was intrigued with her and curious to see just what she would do if I remained still and allowed her the freedom of the camp. Since I was clad only in a pair of shorts, I reasoned that if the worst happened and I got sprayed, the job of cleansing myself would not be too great and, fearfully I must admit, I held my ground.

Matilda came right up to me, sniffed at my bare feet from a distance of about six inches and then nonchalantly went by me, still looking for food.

I tried moving slowly and she didn't so much as glance in my direction. I became braver; I had food in my pack, which was inside the tent, so I went to it and took some bread from it. Outside again Matilda treated me to a curious glance. I threw a piece of bread in her direction. She sniffed once,

Striped skunk

then hurried to it and gobbled it up, and in this manner she swallowed two whole slices.

At this point I decided I was quite safe with Matilda around provided I didn't give her cause to become afraid of me, so I went back to bed, leaving the light on outside. I slept, and in the morning, rather later than usual because of my lost sleep, I peered outside to find that Matilda had gone home.

The next day was Saturday and the lonely lake at which I was camped received other visitors. A party of fishermen pitched a small tent within sight of my own location; there were four men in the party and that night one of them had to sleep outside the tent, warm enough in his sleeping bag, but open to the inquisitive inspection of forest denizens.

I woke to a crescendo of ear-splitting yells. The manly chorus was close; it came, in fact, from my camping neighbors. It was caused by Matilda! Later I learned the sequence of events; evidently Matilda had found the man in the sleep-

152

ing bag and she had immediately decided that his chest would be an ideal place to stop and rest for a while. Matilda was an average skunk and weighed about four pounds (some weigh as much as ten) and the sudden weight on his chest woke the sleeper. He lifted his head to stare Matilda in the eyes. She became curious and thrust her face closer to the man, whereupon he exploded into back-arching action, flinging Matilda in the air and trying to roll out of the imprisoning sleeping bag.

Of course, Matilda objected and when she landed she was already in the position for "shooting". Her body was bent in a U, that is, her head and her "business end" were both aiming at the threshing figure. She fired, and two thin streams of yellow, sticky fluid emerged, met about twelve inches from the skunk's shooting glands and formed a dense, choking spray which enveloped the man and his sleeping bag.

At this point the victim's three companions emerged hurriedly from the tent and were met by two more evil-smelling broadsides. Matilda that morning routed the camp. All four men ran as fast as they could for the lake and, cold as the water was at that time of the morning, dived in. But their efforts were of no avail. Matilda had done her work well and when they left, the quartet still stank of skunk musk.

Matilda was neither repentant nor perturbed. Next night she appeared at my campsite again, but this time she brought her family with her, three miniature skunks that followed wherever she led. I spent some time feeding them and watching their antics and not once was I in danger of that deadly spray.

Matilda taught me much about skunks, which are probably the most maligned creatures of the wilderness. Whisper "skunk" in the hearing of the average man or woman and you are suddenly left alone in the forest; but there is really no need for this fear of skunks—provided one is careful to move slowly and speak gently, and prepared to stand one's ground without resorting to panic. Skunks are then pleasant, interesting and gentle little creatures.

Skunks range all over North America's temperate regions and they are one of the few wild animals that have thrived with the coming of man. They are carnivorous and a large proportion of their diet is made up of insects. Because of this, they prefer to live in areas that provide woodlands for cover and open fields for choice of diet.

Skunks are night creatures. Daytime is for sleeping and the dark hours are for hunting or scavenging. Male skunks and females without young have several lairs to go to when the sun begins to tinge the eastern sky. The creatures travel slowly and often range too far from their favorite den to return to it before daylight. Sometimes the skunk just selects a likely-looking hollow stump, or rock overhang, in which to sleep. At other times it may move in with a groundhog or with another skunk and no one seems to mind the overcrowding.

If it is disturbed during its nightly wanderings, the skunk hardly speeds up at all, mainly because it just can't go fast. Instead it stops, stamps the ground with its front legs and hisses, or it may growl through clicking teeth. Next, if the threat continues, the bushy tail is erected like a black and white plume, then, in a trice, it adopts the U-shape. From this position it can shoot at a distance of ten feet or more and if the wind is in the right quarter its oily spray can travel as much as twenty feet.

At times, however, the skunk's powerful defense is useless. A very hungry wolf or cougar, an eagle or a snowy owl pressed by starvation, will ignore the foul spray and kill the little stinker. The lynx and the bobcat, even badgers and foxes will attack the skunk at such times. And it has other enemies, too. Fleas, lice, dog ticks, wood ticks and mites suck its blood from the outside; inside, parasites such as flatworms and wireworms and sicknesses such as distemper and rabies prey on the skunk. So its lot is not such a happy one as might be assumed from its unique defense.

Like a domestic cat, the skunk dislikes cold and wet. It is not a true hibernator, in that its body temperature alters only slightly when it curls up in a warm underground den to sleep out the cold of winter. The stay indoors varies. Young skunks den longer than adults, but all come out on mild days to forage for food and this is the time when many skunk pelts are taken by trappers. The animal's fur, though coarse, is valuable and sought after by many trappers; and because food is scarce and under natural conditions skunks have little to worry about, they are careless and will invariably fall victims to almost any form of trap or snare.

Mating for the skunks takes place in late winter, generally in March, when the males are rambling far, despite the cold. Already they have been out almost a month, looking for mates, and when the females come out during the first month of spring, fighting skunks can be seen and heard everywhere.

When mating is done, males and females go their own way again and eight weeks later the little skunks come into the world. Between two and nine young ones are born, depending on the age and condition of the mother. The youngsters are not pretty to look at. They are pink, hairless, wrinkled and seem to have no ears, though their pattern of black and white can already be seen under the skin. But young skunks grow quickly. At three weeks their eyes open and they already have good coats and two weeks or so later they are out walking with their mothers. At eight weeks they no longer suck milk, but eat what Mama brings them and do some hunting of their own, and by autumn they are independent beings, foraging for themselves.

Their diet consists of almost anything edible. Young rabbits, chipmunks, mice, insects of all kinds, birds when they can catch them, eggs, including hen eggs right out from under the hen if necessary, carrion, fish, some vegetables; in fact, name it and the skunks will eat it.

Savage Fangs

It is night in the northland. The moon is full; its yellow light reaches down gently over the forest and is refracted by the deep snow. It is a January moon. A cold moon. It hangs high and makes monsters out of shadows and turns the land, with its green conifers and stark, leafless bushes, into a world of fantasy. Frost creeps into the trees and tears at some of them, making them groan their distress in staccato voices that crack loudly through the forest. Here and there a balsam fir, tired from holding the weight of a coverlet of snow, relaxes its boughs and drops a cascade of fine crystals that glitter in the moonlight as they drop, reflecting a thousand minute colors. There is great beauty here, and great savagery.

A wolverine is crouched under a giant pine. He has just killed a snow hare and has eaten it, but he is still hungry and more than usually bad tempered tonight. He sits humped, like the giant weasel that he is, a forty-pound killer who struts to do war on every living thing in the wilderness and fears nothing. His mien is both fascinating and terrifying as he glowers at the world with gaping, bear-like mouth that shows glistening fangs. He moves, seeking another victim, and though he is lithe as he walks, his thick, bowed legs give him a lumbering gait. He has long fur, coarse and shaggy, and because this is winter, stiff hairs protect the soles of his feet, enabling him to walk great distances in the subzero cold.

In the distance the snarl of wolves bickering over a deer carcass reaches the killer. He stops and his small, rounded ears prick forward, pinpointing the sound, and the short muzzle with its keen nose lifts to test the air for scent. Then he moves again, hurrying, and soon, on the border of a small lake, the wolverine sees his quarry. Three large timber wolves are pulling at the body of an old mule deer doe. They are too busy to hear or smell the wolverine until he is almost upon them.

The hair on the creature's back, and on his neck, stands straight. His bushy tail is erected and from his mouth comes a growl that seems too big for his body. He is the essence of ferocity as he advances, head held low, lips drawn back in a wicked snarl, on three fierce animals, each of which outweighs him by some sixty pounds. He seems to be strutting to his death and yet, snarling protest, the great wolves retreat before him. One, bolder than the others, lingers a moment near the deer carcass and the wolverine, growling again, slithers towards it, a bundle of enraged, fighting fury. The wolf turns and runs.

If the wolverine has an enemy it is hunger. For his size the small warrior is the strongest, most ferocious creature of the north woods, and even the cougar and the great, shaggy grizzly bear will retreat before the four-foot-long terror; but nature, as if realizing that she had created too perfect a fighting machine, turned the wolverine's stomach into a weakness. Because the always-moving, quick body consumes energy at a more than usually rapid rate, the wolverine is ever hungry and must satisfy his hunger, especially in winter, or die of weakness. Despite his cunning, his enormous strength, his courage in battle and his endurance against cold and fatigue, hunger also kills the wolverine by depleting his energies and making him vulnerable to attacks from other predators and to the many parasites and microbes the beast harbors in his body.

Tonight, however, the wolverine is safe. He has already eaten a hare, now he has an almost entire deer to devour and he wastes no time. He gorges until his demanding stomach is a round, tight drum, then he moves away slowly, looking for a place in which to sleep off the feast. He finds a bedroom near. It is inside the hollow of a downed pine and there is just room enough for his rotund body. He will stay in this area for two or three days, until he has finished the deer car-

Wolverine

cass, and woe to the animal foolhardy enough to try to steal that which the wolverine himself has stolen! The gluttonous robber will not tolerate the same treatment he metes out to others and, being the creature that he is, he can make his own laws in the northland. Even if he should decide to seek a change of diet, he will not leave meat for others. If, as to-night, he is feeding on a large animal and he does not finish it all, he will tear the remains into small pieces and will store each piece in a different place, to be eaten later, no matter in what condition it may be; having such a large appetite, the wolverine is not choosy. He eats fresh meat or rotten meat and will devour frogs and snails. He stalks and kills ground birds, such as grouse and ptarmigan, and goes after even the smallest rodents.

Night has fled before the sun. A gray jay, inquisitive and cheeky, flies squawking over the remains of the deer and droplands on the carcass. The bird peers about, seeking danger and seeing none; it pulls at the meat, taking morsels of fat from it and swallowing them with quick, jerky movements of its head and outstretched neck. Four times it dips its beak and pulls free some food, then the wolverine's growl of rage reaches the bird. It knows the sound and it lifts its streamlined body into the topmost boughs of a spruce. From its high perch it squawks at the wolverine, which is even then breakfasting on the deer.

A strong, musky odor permeates the frosty air this morning. It was not evident here last night. It comes from the wolverine, from two glands under his tail, which, when he is excited, produce a foul discharge, as strong as the musk spray of a skunk. The creature's smell came when he saw the jay picking at his meat and now the carcass is tainted with it, safe from all but the wolverine himself.

January and February have faded into March and the snow is crusted with the ice of daytime thaws which have frozen during the cold of night. The wolverine is thinking less of his stomach today, for he wants a mate. For the first time in eleven months he feels alone. Like all of his breed he is normally a solitary creature, too surly to be content with the duties of companionship, too fierce to tolerate interference, too greedy to share. But during this last month of winter, the wolverine feels the urge of kinship and he ranges far, smelling at likely places, studying the ground for tracks, and listening for echoes of a fearful growl such as his own.

It is early afternoon and the sun, which has become stronger with the retreat of winter, is favoring a small valley with the comfort of its warmth. Steam is rising from the boles of the pines and small droplets of snow water fall now and then from the pale green needles that dress the branches. A willow bush, already showing tinges of orange that speak of sap be-

159

ginning its journey of life beneath the bark, is crusted with ice. The sun shines on the laden branches and the ice coating has taken the clarity of crystal.

Near the willow there is a dark brown shape. It is still, except for the even movements of its flanks. The she-wolverine is watching the male as he lumbers into the valley, drawn there by the scent of her. Even in courtship, the creatures are savage. They greet each other with evil growls and stay together just long enough for the male to deposit his seed inside the female. They will be strangers from then on.

The male leaves the valley. The female stays, making short forays in the area but always returning at night to a hole she has found under an immense boulder. She will remain here until she gives birth to two or three, perhaps as many as five, young ones. The cubs may be light brown, buff, or even white, and they will have dark bands along their sides; not until later, in the autumn, when their mother leaves them to forage for themselves, will they take on the hues of adults and by then they will be almost fully grown.

The male, meanwhile, hunts, kills, steals and eats endlessly. Three days after leaving his mate he finds a mink caught in an iron trap; he eats the mink, notices faint signs in the snow and trails them and finds another trap. He eats the snowshoe hare that it contains and continues following the trapline. By evening he has cleared every trap of its victim and has ruined two days' work for the trapper.

Night after night he visits the traps and eats the animals they contain. Night after night he skillfully avoids the traps set for him by the desperate trapper. Beaver, muskrat, mink, weasel, hare, once a lynx, another time a wolf strangled in a steel snare, nothing can stop the cunning raider. The trapper now puts out snares for the thief, who steals the bait, first springing the trap by turning it over in the snow and dragging it until the trigger that is hooked into the bait pan is released. When the bait is gone, the robber tears the trap free of its mooring and hides it.

The trapper gives up. It is now almost spring and he has had a good season, so he gathers his traps and pulls out for the settlement.

160

Happy Bandits

The river was still. It was a wide, deep waterway that thread-
ed its lazy way between pine-clad mountains and picked up
speed when it turned on its course and began to run downhill
towards the lowlands. Here, where it flowed through the center of a low valley, it looked like a band of burnished silver,
reflecting the blue sky and the trees and trapping small lances
of sun. The river's west bank was steep and rock-studded and
was now in shadow, for the afternoon was old and the lowering sun was shining behind the tree-tops, lighting only the flat
east bank.

On the shadowy side of the water the trout were feeding;
the fish were not very hungry yet, but some of them could
not resist rising to take an unwary insect as it brushed the
quiet surface. Soft splashes signaled the trout's rising, and
multiplying circles on the water showed where they had
been. High in the sky, a golden eagle planed slow circles as
it scanned its territory for prey. In a great poplar on the east
bank a pileated woodpecker was excavating oblong holes in
one of the tree's giant limbs, dead years before and now the
home of ants and other insects which were food to the large
black and white bird with the red crest; the woodpecker's
powerful beak made loud drumming noises on the dry wood
and white chips fell to the grass below.

The otter sat near the poplar. His rich, brown coat blended
perfectly with the shadows of the willow bush under which
he squatted. He had fed earlier that day, diving into the
glossy waters and catching two large rainbow trout; he was
not really hungry just now, but he had been watching the

splashes and circles made by the hunting fish and the thought of his favorite food tempted him to slide back into the river and get just one more fish. One of the wood chips fell near his nose and this seemed to annoy him. He looked up into the tree and barked at the woodpecker, a short, dry whoof of irritation, then, casting one wary look up high, at the sailing eagle, he got to his feet and waddled towards the water.

As soon as the brown body moved in the grass, the great eagle changed course and started a circle over the otter, but the distance to the water was too short to allow him to dive on his prey. The otter knew this and risked his move. The sky hunter gave up and returned to his patient quest for other food.

The otter swam north, parallel to the east bank for several yards, until he came to an old, waterlogged pine that was anchored by mud to the bank. Beside this he submerged, quietly, and at once sank to the muddy bottom. He crept along slowly, just inches off the mud, propelling himself with his powerful tail and his webbed back feet, making his way towards the west bank, where the trout were feeding. His fur, chocolate-brown when dry, was now heavy with water and had turned almost black, making his slowly-moving outline almost invisible as he inched his way across the river bottom.

Reaching the murk of the west bank he turned on his side, slowly, with infinite caution, and scanned the upper water. Six feet away, floating placidly above him, was a large rainbow trout, its streamlined head facing into the current, its tail flukes waving slowly from side to side to keep itself anchored against the flow of the river. The big fish was resting in the cool depth; it was not one of the ones darting up to grasp dragonfly or mosquito from the roof of the water. The otter moved again. Imperceptibly his sleek, seal-like body came closer to the fish.

Suddenly, with quick threshing of the round tail and powerful thrusts of the short back legs, the otter darted upwards, a dark streak that cleaved through the water, releasing some of the air particles trapped in its fur so that a silver stream of tiny bubbles formed a liquid V around his body. Too late the trout tried to rear away. In an instant the otter's mouth opened, the needle-sharp canine teeth fastened on the fish and the victor paddled slowly to the surface, staying close to the shadow bank, remembering the soaring eagle.

Nearby, wedged between two rocks, was a sloping game trail; here came deer and moose, and timber wolves and foxes, and raccoons and bear, using the trail as their kind had done for centuries, to drink of the cool, clear river water. The otter used the slope now. Waddling up it on legs that on land looked too short for his four-foot-long body, he reached the top, turned right and sought the sanctuary of a downed red pine. Under the canopy of brown branches the dog ate his fish, afterwards wiping his front paws and his face on the green grass; then he went to sleep, stretched on his side, his hand-like front paws curled into small fists and pressed tight against his chest.

Half a mile away from the dog otter, on the same river but farther up its course, there was a narrow reach that was heavily shaded by the branches of oak and cottonwood and maple and further protected by tall evergreens that grew in thick clusters on either side of the water. The trees nearest the water's edge leaned towards each other and their longest branches spanned the gap and touched twenty feet above the river, forming a canopy of green and shade, and concealment. Five dark objects were gliding smoothly over the water, going in fast circles, always remaining in the center of the river; now and then one of them disappeared suddenly and came into view again moments later in a different place. It was the bitch otter and her four kits, little, frolicsome creatures that were having their first real outing since the day, nearly five weeks before, when they were born in the old muskrat den on the east bank of the river.

Now they were miniature replicas of their mother, but on the day of their birth they were tiny, round and blind, mewing plaintively like small, hoarse kittens as they suckled at their mother's milk. Today they were still darker than their mother, but five weeks ago they were almost black and their fur was thin, just a first protective covering given to them by creation. Sixty days before their birth, during early March, when the snow still lay heavy on the ground and only the center of the river was free of ice, the bitch and the dog mated in the quiet of the bushes, remained together for a short time and then parted company, the dog seeking new mates, the bitch looking for a den.

When she discovered the muskrat burrow on the river bank the rat was still living in it. She waited for him to come out one fine morning when the sun was melting the river ice, and when he did she pounced and killed him, eating of his carcass; then she enlarged his den, scooping out a round chamber at the end of it for herself and her brood.

When the kits were born towards the end of April they each weighed a little less than half a pound. Three males and one female were born to the young mother, which was a good number, for some mothers have only one or two, and most have three. The little ones, like all otter young, were slow to develop and could not see until they were over one month old. Yesterday they had left their den for the first time and the mother had led them to the shallow water and started teaching them how to swim; today they were still learning, but now they could go into the deep and dive and play under water for minutes at a time and they were enjoying themselves as only young otters can.

They are frivolous creatures, these otters. They love life and they love play, even the old ones. They spend hours at a time sliding down a mud bank into the water, lying on their bellies, their short legs pointing backwards, their sharp seal-like faces looking down and their tails dragging behind. In winter, when the earth is frozen, they may come to the same bank and use the snow to toboggan onto the lake, their bodies cushioned by the deep white blanket that lies on the ice.

This carefree, happy bandit is as much at home in the water as he is on land; under the surface, the otter can swim a quarter of a mile without taking a breath and he can streak after fish faster than the fish themselves can swim. Weather does not bother him. Winter or spring, summer or autumn, it is all one to the otter. He keeps cool in the hot weather by taking frequent baths, and warm in the winter because under

River otter

his skin there is a layer of fat that gives him perfect insulation
against the frost, while on the outside he wears a coat of
short, thick fur close to his body and a quilt of long, shiny-
tipped guardhairs.

On this day the mother has taken her young out of the water and they are shaking themselves on the bank, close to
their den; always when the otters leave the water they shake
their sleek coats first and then roll in the grass or the snow,
drying off most of their wetness; in this way they groom
themselves and keep their fur from freezing during the cold
months. The bitch draws one of the kits to her and starts
combing out its fur, beginning at its head and working on
down the back, along the belly and right up to the tail. She
talks to her baby as she works, mumbling constantly in her
hoarse voice. Once she digs too deep into the young skin;
the little otter whines protest and the mother barks, as
though in apology. Later on, when the kits grow older, they
will take turns to groom each other and some of them will
comb their mother's fur.

A soft summer evening spills small winds over the moonlit river during the month of August and the otter family is busy hunting, seeking first its favorite food, fish. The little otters have grown to half the size of their eighteen-pound mother and they are always hungry and range alone or with their family in a constant search for food. If, as tonight, they cannot catch enough fish to satisfy their hunger, almost anything else will do, including ducks or other water birds, muskrats or beaver, snails or crayfish, insects or frogs. When a fish is caught, the otter eats it headfirst, so that the sharp, backward-spreading bones will pass harmlessly through its digestive system, and just before the fish disappears whole down its throat, the otter bites off the tail.

Under the moon the river shines silver, a moving, splashing mirror that is full of the sounds of night. A raccoon, pausing on the east bank to drink, hears the otters and chitters to her young, warning them to be careful, for though the big old mother is safe from the otters, the young raccoons will make a tasty meal if they are careless and become separated from their defender. On the far bank the dog otter, just coming to play with his family, hears the raccoon and wonders for a moment if it will be worth while to cross the river and try to catch one of the young ones; but memory of another night, when he tried this and found himself face to face with a furious old coon, makes him change his mind and he slides into the water and joins his family.

His Ninth Life

Four thousand feet up the flanks of a mountain in British Columbia there is an abandoned mining camp; the jumble of fallen wooden buildings nestles on a flat shelf and is surrounded by young fir trees. One of these buildings, a long gray structure that was once the mess hall, has slipped from its moorings and lies drunkenly in a shallow ravine; its roof has slipped to one side and the cedar shingles that once covered it lie in an untidy pile, some of them still adhering to boards. Beneath this pile of debris lives a colony of marmots, plump, curious creatures that inhabited the area even before the last miner turned his back on the empty mountain and left to seek gold elsewhere.

The marmots are food to the big cat that is slowly climbing towards the flat shelf. The creature's pace, as usual, is deliberate, cautious. He walks low, crouching and seeking the concealment of fallen trees and bushes, but now and then he stops and raises himself on legs that are surprisingly long for such a short-bodied animal. Standing at full height he scans the area around him with piercing, yellow eyes; there is no prey in sight and the cat plods on, inching his lithe body upwards, traveling a hunting trail he has used for three seasons, since he first discovered the marmot colony under the old mine buildings.

It won't be light on the mountain for a time yet, not until the sun has shed yellow over the world that lies on the other side of it, but this matters little to the lynx, whose eyes were made for night. He is a dark-prowler and the pupils of his eyes expand greatly during the hours after the sun has set,

Lynx

capturing even the slightest light; in the day the pupils are reduced to mere black slits.

The lynx started hunting late last night. He lives in a small valley between this mountain and the next, usually sleeping in the hollow of a big pine log. Yesterday he fed well, pulling down four grouse in a thicket of firs; with a full belly and thirst quenched at a nearby stream, the cat slept late, lazing in his shelter until the sun was gone and blackness filled the mountains, for the moon was not to rise until several hours later.

Perhaps the lynx thought of the marmots and was too lazy then to climb the steep path to their home range, or perhaps he followed a whim and stayed in his own back yard, hoping to find a hare or two, or one of last spring's fawns. Whatever the reason, he stayed and prowled and failed to catch even a mouse and now, hungry, tired and bad tempered, he was going after the marmots.

Somewhere deep in the recesses of his mind there was an uneasy fear. Hitherto he had had little difficulty in finding and killing at least one snowshoe hare during a night's hunting. But then things changed and the hares became scarcer and now, this summer, they had become difficult to locate and this was bad, for the lynx depends on the snowshoe hare for most of his living. When the hares go into their periodic decline, the lynx and many other carnivores must leave their hunting grounds in search of new prey or perish of hunger the following winter. Because of his fear and his hunger, he was more than usually savage as he neared the home of the marmots.

There was a grayness at the mine site. He stopped on the trail, using his nose and his ears and his great eyes to probe the decaying buildings, and quickly he spotted a large, dark brown marmot. The rodent was beside its hole; it sat upright, holding its front paws against its chest, and scanned the area, wondering if it dared to go a little way from its bolt-hole in search of some of the more tender grasses. The lynx froze into a crouch. His shoulder blades and his hips protruded above his back, his powerful hind legs were bunched under his body, his front legs with their great paws and razor claws spread before him.

The marmot sniffed at the dawn; it peered hard in all directions and wiggled its ears, seeking to pick up signs of danger. In another moment it decided there was nothing to fear ten feet away from its hole, and it dropped to four legs and scuttled along the ground towards a patch of grass and sow thistles that grew where once a shed had stood. The lynx watched, tense but patient, waiting until the marmot settled to its feed. Ten minutes elapsed and the marmot was busy eating. Now and then it stopped, raised itself on its back legs and had a look around, then it resumed its munching of the grass. The cat began inching towards his prey, dragging his thirty-pound body over the rough ground, taking advantage of whatever cover he could find. Of recent months, because game was becoming scarce, the lynx had done most of his hunting this way, stalking patiently until he was in position for the last swift rush that would propel his body onto hare or bird, crushing the victim by his weight and making one quick bite with his curved fangs to sever the spinal column just at the base of the skull. In the past, when the hares were plentiful, the cat often lay in wait for a victim, stretched concealed over a log or a rock ledge, ready to drop on the first small creature that passed under him.

Now, just as the lynx bunched for his leap, a short, softly-sharp whistle broke the stillness around the old mine camp; another marmot had seen the hunter and was warning its fellows. But the warning came too late for the fat creature eating grass. As he prepared to dash for the safety of his burrow, the cat's body flashed through space and landed on the terrified victim. In a moment it was over and the lynx rose with the body of the marmot gripped between his teeth. He dragged the three-pound carcass away from the camp and settled to his meal in the shelter of a downed fir.

The wilderness is blooming when the young lynxes are born; it is May and the forest is basking in the warmth of spring. In the shelter of a deadfall, or under piled rocks, one to four kittens are born to the mother cat sixty days after her mating during the late winter. The little ones look somewhat like house-cat kittens, but they are a little larger and much more handsome, with reddish or buff coats streaked and mottled with fawn. They are blind until they are about ten days old, then their eyes open and they skitter about the den and play with each other, like their domestic cousins. Already they have the long legs of their breed and the short, black-tipped tail, and the big feet which, by winter, will have grown long, coarse hair that will allow the lynxes to walk over the deep snow.

For the first two months of their lives the kittens romp and suck milk from their mother and chew little pieces of the meat she brings home for them. Then they start going out with the she-cat to learn the ways of the wilderness and practice the hunting skills with which they have been born and which they have already started using in their games. Soon after, the mother begins to wean her young; her lessons become longer and the kittens are expected to start catching things, small creatures at first, like mice, or the small, rabbit-like animals called pikas that live in the western mountains. Already the happy time of youth is fading for the cats and by winter they will be turned away from the nursery to fend for themselves.

By autumn the young cats have put on their winter over-coats of beautiful pastel-shaded gray fur, about four inches long. Already they are husky and well able to take care of themselves, weighing eighteen or twenty pounds. They have few enemies, for only the wolverine dares to face an adult lynx. With their tufted ears, thick ruff, long legs and big feet, they are handsome creatures, not as bad tempered as their bobcat cousins, but indomitable fighters who can always pro-tect their rights, except perhaps against another, bigger lynx.

Summer was a trying time for the lynx. The snowshoe hares had all but disappeared and the pikas and chipmunks seemed to have followed them; even the squirrels were scarce. Early one morning, the big lynx pounced on a red fox as it was trotting down-mountain and that day he fed well, for he was not squeamish and ignored the strong, musky odor of the fox. But hunting had become a hazardous task and even the marmot colony had been cut down by the dep-redations of the lynx and other meat eaters.

One night the lynx smelled deer. Three white-tails were ambling up the mountain and the cat tried to pull one down, for when game is scarce this courageous beast will attack al-most any animal, except, of course, such giants as the moose and the elk. But the deer smelled the cat, and bolted.

Once, two years ago, he had killed a deer. He had sur-prised a two-year-old buck as it was feeding on the mountain-side and he had jumped for the neck, landing with claws bared, cutting into the terrified white-tail's hide with his sharp hooks. While the frantic buck charged away, down-trail, the lynx began biting through the tough skin and muscle protect-ing the jugular vein and he reached the pulsing blood supply before the buck was able to dash his enemy against a tree.

The cat was lucky that night; it is not often that a lynx can kill an adult deer and get away unhurt.

That September the cat made one last visit to the old mine site. Not a single marmot was there and the lynx knew then that he must move out of this area or face starvation in the snows of winter. Twitching his stump of a tail, he padded away from the collapsed mess hall and turned down-trail, aiming for the flatlands and the heavy forest area where he hoped to find more game; he had to have food, live food, not carrion, but he was not one to pick and choose over his choice of victim. Hares and rabbits were his staff of life, but if they were not available birds, squirrels, foxes, or even skunks would do and if he could not get these, then deer or mountain sheep and perhaps a coyote or two, if he could take them by surprise and drop on them from the height of a tree perch.

In the valley the snow drifted into great white dunes that were packed hard by a biting, subzero wind; it was early March and the winter had been severe and the lynx had gone hungry often. Now he was rangy, bad tempered and looking for a mate, for it was the breeding time. This night he stood in the lower branches of an old pine and stared at the darkness, his black-tipped ears moving in search of sound, his pug nose sniffing at the wind. Suddenly he opened his mouth and emitted a dreadful cry. It was a scream of passion, an intense, rending yell that burst from his throat and launched itself into the night to terrify all small creatures within a mile of the sound. Again and again the tom-cat screamed his unearthly call, then he stopped as suddenly as he had started, and he listened.

In moments an answering wail reached him. He immediately launched into his own furious howl and the night was made hideous by the great cries of two male lynxes, rivals ready to tear each other to pieces for the favor of a female. The weird duet lasted for almost fifteen minutes, then the tom-cat jumped down from the pine and went in search of his enemy. Somewhere in the dark was a young she-cat and the tom meant to mate with her. But first the intruder in his territory had to be driven out, or killed if he would not leave.

The two toms met in a small clearing. The intruder was younger and smaller, probably one of last summer's kittens, now out to fulfil himself. They stood about ten yards apart and stared at each other, their ridiculously short tails swishing from side to side and low growls coming from their ruffed throats. Stiff-legged they advanced and when only five or six feet separated them the older tom screamed fury and charged. He hit the young cat on the flank, knocked him down and was upon him, rending with front talons while the heavier claws on the back legs raked at the soft, white belly. The attack was too furious, too damaging for the young cat. Screaming rage and pain he squirmed out from under his opponent and fled into the trees while the winner stormed about the clearing, meowing and growling, boasting of his deed.

Later that same night the tom met the she-cat and they mated. When it was over he left, perhaps to seek a new mate, perhaps on the prowl for rabbit or hare. He was still traveling by morning when the trapper saw him, aimed his gun and shot him through the head.

The big lynx lay on his side, dead. But it did not really matter now, for he had left his seed behind.

The Hungry Night

A smiling harvest moon beamed over the forest. Beneath the heavens the green woods were silent. Almost. The daytime bustle was gone and the birds were quiet, but here and there, under a brush pile or deep inside a cluster of ferns, small rustling sounds excited the watcher to a pitch of frenzied impatience.

His compact body was bunched upon a small mound that overlooked the forest floor. Towering above the mound, majestic pines cast dappled shadows that hindered the keen eyes of the watcher as they swept the terrain.

The short, tufted ears moved in jerky sweeps, combining their motion with the searching eyes as the watcher attempted to pinpoint a sound that was more persistent and closer than the rest.

Its movement concealed by the mound, a short, bobbed tail brushed over the grass in constant motion, the only physical sign of the cat's impatience.

The bobcat was hungry. He was a big, young tom in prime condition, except for an almost healed wound on his right shoulder that had been inflicted on him by the old male that had inhabited this area of forest three weeks before.

Early one morning the young cat had come strolling into the glen he was now watching, looking for a place to settle. Unaware of the baleful eyes that were fixed on his casual approach, he had paused by a hare "form" seeking to learn whether it still served as home for a snowshoe. He had decided the form was abandoned and had opened his mouth to yawn in replete boredom—he had pulled down and feasted on two fat grouse the night before—when the old cat charged, snarling defiance.

The fight had been noisy, but short. The old cat had the advantage of weight, but the intruder was quicker and healthier, and his teeth and claws, unlike the age-worn weapons of his adversary, were like rapiers in the hands of an experienced swordsman.

He killed the old cat. Afterwards, when he had finished licking his wound, he slept. That night he returned to the body of his enemy and ate of it. He stayed near the carcass for three days and nights and when he left it to again hunt smaller prey only some blood-streaked skin and a few mounds of scattered, dark brown fur remained.

The wound was deep and painful and though the bobcat would have preferred the meat of a young rabbit, he had been glad of the old tom's carcass. It allowed him to rest his shoulder and to recuperate his strength.

In the three weeks since the fight the bobcat had gone hungry more often than he had satisfied his craving for meat; the wound made him stiff and shortened the fierce hunting rushes that would normally have propelled him in seven-foot leaps onto the back of his unsuspecting prey.

When he was born fifty days after his mother had mated with his father he was the smallest of three kittens and the last to greet the gloomy granite of the rock cave his mother had used as a den.

But nature helped him. His brother died when he was eight days old, the day before he and his sister opened their eyes. A week later his sister crawled to the cave opening and rolled out.

The mother cat was out hunting and the young tom was about to follow his sister when a swift shadow darkened the den opening. There was a rustle of wings and one startled, pain-filled cry from his sister, then she was gone, carried high towards the eyrie, stifled and pierced by the talons of the eagle.

The tom, a puny being until then, gorged on his mother's milk, grew strong and, in June, left the den with the she-cat on his first hunting trip. He weighed five pounds that day

Bobcat

and had not yet become imbued with the anger that would drive him until some day another, stronger cat would come to take from him that which he had usurped from the old cat of the glen.

But none of this concerned the tom tonight. Now he was king; tomorrow was of no consequence.

His keen eyes detected a soft movement in the glen. He froze, concentrating all his powers on the shadows that wreathed the base of a sprawling young maple bush. His ears picked up clearer sound and flashed it to the small brain that was already interpreting the message delivered by the amber eyes.

Twenty feet away, the cat's mind computed, a feeding rabbit was edging out of the shelter of the maple bush. It was moving towards the mound upon which the tom crouched, incautiously heading with the wind.

The tom's nostrils had been busy analyzing the scents of the night; rabbit taint was everywhere, but now the cat could isolate the smell of this one rodent.

Carefully he bunched his powerful back legs, tensing nervously for the first leap.

The rabbit moved again, closer. The cat's body became immobile for a fraction of time, then it surged through the air, back legs trailing the stocky body, the square head held high and the front legs, their powerful claws unsheathed, reaching for the victim.

But hunger had spoiled the cat's judgment. His leap had been made too soon and even before he landed the rabbit was turning in frantic haste. The bobcat's front paws touched the earth and almost before his back quarters settled on the ground his body bunched and was lifted again into arcing flight.

He landed nearly eight feet away, almost on top of the maple bush, and he heard the escaping rush of the rabbit.

The cat didn't leap again. His body with its narrow chest and small lungs was not capable of the sustained speed necessary to overtake the fleeing quarry, and he knew this.

Now there was real silence in the glen. The bobcat had alerted the forest and he would have to wait for new prey.

He growled, a low sound from deep in his throat. The bobbed tail jerked angrily from side to side as he turned and padded away from the scene of his defeat.

He peered once at the full moon, blinked at its yellow light and stalked away, heading for the deep bush.

This was to be his night of hunger.

Three-Toes

Red sunlight splashes the canyon floor. A light summer breeze stirs the evergreens, tousling their branches and plucking from them soft notes which blend into a gentle bushland symphony. A flock of ruffed grouse twitter as the birds shuffle into comfort on their roosting places in the lower arms of a tamarack. Beyond a dense belt of spruce a small herd of white-tailed deer are grazing in a clearing, pulling contentedly at the long grass but, as usual, nervously alert, their big ears flapping and swiveling, probing the evening air in a constant search for danger signals.

The buck is a handsome fellow. He carries his antlers regally as he stands a little apart from the smaller does and between mouthfuls of grass he pauses, holding his massive head high and flaring his black nostrils to test the wind for warning smells from down-canyon. The buck is nervous; he senses trouble, but is unsure of its direction and he moves undecided on long, slim legs that cover the ground in jerky strides and take him closer to the tree line.

The evening is quiet, its sounds seemingly innocent: the scrunch of bitten grass, the occasional flutter of a grouse, the rustle of wind-tossed leaves.

Suddenly a squirrel shrills in sharp anger and the buck freezes into a tense crouch, ready to leap away and lead his does to the safety of the trees. The squirrel, a red shape sitting in a young spruce, bunches his body into a small ball of fur and continues his chatter, a note of fear creeping into his petulant voice. But the buck is not yet sure, despite the squirrel's warning. Danger is about, and he knows it, but he must locate it before he can run from it.

The does are less alert, confident in his ability to protect them; they continue eating, glancing now and then towards him, waiting for his decision, and their erratic movements take them farther from the tree line and closer to an outcropping of rock which rises fifteen feet above ground.

Unseen and silent, a tawny shape slides stealthily between tufted blueberry bushes. The big cat moves imperceptibly, inching forward and pausing often to stare with baleful unblinking eyes at the squirrel. The cougar has not eaten for three days, and though her two kittens suckled milk an hour before from her almost-dry dugs, they, too, are hungry and wait mewling in the cave that still serves them as home. Because of her need to provide for the kittens the cougar is more than usually careful this evening as she stalks the deer, subduing the eagerness that urges her to dash headlong into the band. She is downwind from the herd and safe from detection provided she is careful, and the rocky ledge offers a good jumping-off platform that will let her land within striking reach of at least one of the animals.

A young doe edges closer to the outcrop. She pulls at some grass, reaching for the green food with her rough tongue, curling it around a tuft and drawing it into her mouth; the doe moves again, unaware that death lurks above. Seventy-five feet separate her from the hungry cat who is nervously bunching her powerful haunches, positioning her back legs for the mighty leap.

The time is now. For a split second the yellow body is still, then, like the sudden uncoiling of a mighty spring, her muscles push her off the ledge, propelling the 100-pound body through space. She seems to hang poised in mid-air, long tail arching over her body, legs spread, ready for the landing, but her shadow is a swiftly-traveling blur against the spruce trees.

She touches ground twenty feet short of the young doe, continues her forward movement, brings her back legs down and forward until they are positioned between her front legs. She springs again and hits the deer and the deadly front paws strike the doe's shoulder and drive her front quarters away from the cat; the unexpected force of the powerful blow snaps the deer's neck forward. The crack of breaking bone is heard a fraction of a second before the doe is hurtled to the ground fifteen feet away from where she was hit. The deer is dead before she knows what has happened.

The rest of the herd streak away to the safety of the evergreens, white tails bobbing like pennants, the buck's snort of fear sounding above the sharp clattering of hoofs. The cougar watches them go, swishing her tail from side to side, her head turned at right angles to her body, and she looses a low, gruff growl.

When all sound of the fleeing herd is muffled by the evergreens the cougar pads over to the kill; she snuffles at the warm carcass, nudging it with her muzzle, then she reaches out with one front paw and rips at the doe's stomach. Her movements are swift and expert, but fastidious, rather like those of a particularly fussy house cat hooking a tidbit of meat from a plate.

She begins to eat and slowly her gaunt haunches fill out as she pulls at the warm meat, her yellow jaws stained pink. When she has finished there are almost eight pounds of meat in her belly and she thinks of her young. By now dusk has settled over the mountains. It is the quiet time of shadows, the time when the things of day give way to the creatures of dark; the time when silence can be heard and slight noises are able to travel great distances and become a language that the night beasts hear and heed.

The cougar stands over her kill. A rumbling gurgle travels through her stomach and becomes a hoarse belch as it is released through her mouth. The big cat yawns, stretches her long, supple body and starts dragging the doe's carcass to the edge of the timber line; she handles the dead weight easily and soon drops it under the canopy of a hemlock. With her paws she drags leaves and mulch over the remains, caching the food that will last her some six days, unless marauders find it while she is away caring for her kittens.

Before the arrival of her young she would have settled down for the night near her kill, secure in the knowledge that she had nothing to fear. Man and his howling dogs are

Cougar

---

her only enemies, but now she is far from them, hidden by the immense world of gorges and peaks, of craggy canyons and steep mountain slopes, where she is queen, respected even by the huge, cross grizzly bears that share her domain.

The cougar learned young to fear man. She met the creature once in the foothill country and one of his bullets found her left front paw, ripping off two of her toes. That was three years ago, when she was an inexperienced two-year-old and not long after she and her brother had been chased away by a mother who was heavy with new life and could no longer be responsible for her large children.

At first the young cats had tried to follow the mother but the old she turned on them, a spitting, slashing fury that would have destroyed them both if they had not fled from her; from that time on the mother was a stranger, fierce and jealous for the new litter she would soon raise. Such is the way of the big cats. This one had taught her cubs well, now it was time for them to go and, in the face of her fury, they understood.

Like all males of the cat family the tom was lazy, always ready to eat of a kill but seldom troubling himself to help in the killing. He followed his sister, content to let her lead, but for several days after they left their mother the cats went hungry. Deer were scarce that year and the she-cat had to make do with an occasional cottontail and, once, an old fox, grown careless through age and defective hearing.

Gradually the lions worked their way out of the mountain, down into the foothills. It was a day of early summer when they first smelled man. Three-toes took her brother down from the heights and reached the grasslands just as the cattle stirred awake. She heard them and smelled the strong odor of them long before the two cats reached the line fence that marked the end of the wilderness and the beginning of man's domain. Though she paused suspiciously when she saw the alien fenceposts and barbed wire, hunger drove her forward, against the warning instincts that spoke of hidden dangers.

When she reached the fence her nostrils detected a disquieting scent. She had not smelled this before, and it made her afraid, yet her hunger was acute and her senses told her that out there, almost hidden by the lush pasture, was food that would be easy to take. She bellied under the last strand of wire, followed by the less cautious tom, and as they started pushing their way through the alfalfa the bellow of a yearling calf sounded near. Three-toes blended her body into the ground and the tom imitated her. Moments later she made the kill, while the tom, excited by the nearness of so many cattle, charged the herd, scattering them in bellowing panic across the plain but failing to reach any of the animals. After a short chase his small lungs labored so hard within his narrow chest that he was forced to give up. He loped back to where his sister was already feeding on the Hereford and the two lions gorged, eating most of the warm intestines and some of the ribs and loin. When they finished Three-toes looked for a place in which to sleep off the feed. The prairie offered poor cover so she led her brother into the hills, to a

182

rocky overhang protected by bushy willow growth.

It was there that the hunter's dogs startled them and led them the chase of death, a chase that only ended when one bullet maimed the she and the big, young tom lay lifeless under the pines, a pack of howling dogs worrying his carcass. It was fortunate for Three-toes that the hunter thought he was chasing only one cougar; when the tom died, the hunt was called off and Three-toes, wounded and in pain, continued climbing, seeking the sanctuary of her lonely mountains.

Crippled and hungry, Three-toes took refuge in a cave and stayed there for five days; when she emerged she was gaunt and savagely bad tempered, but though her foot was healing she had to still her hunger with carrion left by other hunters and as a result she didn't mate that year. Several times male cougars came courting her, whistling their strange, bird-like call and leaving scratchings of bare earth upon which they deposited their scent for her, but Three-toes ignored them. Cougars don't mate regularly, as most other mammals do, and the she-cat had other things to worry about that year.

Eventually her paw healed and she hunted again, regaining her lost strength, but she had learned her lesson. Never again would she pad down from the highlands to venture into the territory of man.

One spring, while she was dozing on a flat rock, enjoying the sunny warmth of the early day, Three-toes again heard the plaintive whistle of a tom. Her short ears pricked forward and she sat up.

Suddenly the day's quiet was shattered by an intense, shrill scream that ended in a hoarse cough; Three-toes was replying to the male. After the scream she bounded off the rock and loped into the trees, new emotions stirring within her. When she found the male's scratching place she stopped and sniffed at it and she screamed again, a fearsome wail seldom heard by human ears.

For two weeks Three-toes and the tom courted, then he left. Three months later, in early August, she gave birth to her first litter of three blind, furry kittens. The youngsters were quite unlike their parents; their yellow coats were spotted with dark brown. At birth they measured little more than twelve inches and they weighed about fourteen ounces each.

As her mother had done before her, Three-toes fed and trained her kittens until they were almost two years old, then, another whistle and the odor of fresh scratchings re-awakened her mating urges and she left the young cougars. Tonight she is going to feed her second litter; the two babies are waiting for her in the cave.

Turning her back on the hidden deer carcass she moves away through the trees, a long, yellow blur, at peace with herself and the world in which she dwells.

Curious Cats

Only twice have I ever seen a wild ocelot and only once did I see a jaguarundi in its natural habitat. Because of this I must make it clear that I am no field expert where these two interesting felines are concerned. I have, of course, observed them in captivity on numerous occasions and I have read much about them and talked with people who know them relatively well. But because captivity changes the habits of animals and because second-hand knowledge offers many pitfalls to the naturalist-writer, I dare not do much more than record here my own sketchy experiences with these animals and back them up as best I can with the material gleaned from others.

Some years ago I set out in a battered Land Rover with the intention of driving from western Canada to Venezuela, primarily to study as much wildlife as I could find during the trip, but also to accomplish a journey that was historically of great interest to me. Alas, the trip was never finished. It came to an abrupt end within about fifteen kilometers of Comitan, in south-central Mexico, when the Land Rover up and died. When a piston rod elects to punch a hole clean through an engine block in an area where major mechanical facilities are not available, and when the vehicle has been purchased for $300 Canadian and has since traveled some 6000 miles through roads that were almost certainly built during the height of the Mayan dynasty, even an intrepid naturalist decides that decent burial is about the only service that can be rendered the old crock.

So there I was, facing a fifteen-kilometer hike in the heat

of a Mexican July, when the noise of Carlos' model A truck reached my ears. I turned to look back the way I had come and my eyes detected a great cloud of red dust nearing me at a conservative twenty-five miles per hour. Inside this cloud were Carlos and his dowager machine. He stopped, we talked (I blessed my Spanish mother for giving me her language), and an hour later I was burning holes in my stomach with food served graciously by Conchita, Carlos' buxom and amiable wife, while seven small, brown, very inquisitive children were "driving" the dead Land Rover which Carlos had towed to his red-roofed, whitewashed home.

I have never liked chili peppers, or any other kind of pepper, come to that, but what do you do when a meal is pressed upon you with such good grace, friendliness and expectations that the *señor* will relish your best food? You eat, that's what, and you thank the providence that made you pop into your first-aid can three packages of Rolaids! But this is beside the point. . . .

Carlos turned out to be an entrepreneur. I am not sure just what he did all the time, but he quickly offered to guide me on various trips through the mountains not far from his home, and to house and feed me for two pesos a day and the remains of the Land Rover. Counting my store of Rolaids, I estimated I could last one week before my stomach gave out completely, and because Carlos was so self-assured, professing an intimate knowledge of the flora and fauna of his area—and because they were great people, too!—I accepted his services at the tendered price.

The first day with Carlos as a guide proved two things: he had no idea at all about natural history and he firmly believed that the only way to walk was noisily. To these un-accomplishments he added his great booming voice.

"See, Don Ronaldo, there is a tree!" he would yell at intervals, as though to prove that he knew a tree when he saw one.

On the second day, I set out alone with a tortilla lunch and a bottle of wine, two canteens full of water, my camera equipment and, I am convinced, very little common sense. There were no thermometers around, so I cannot say with

Ocelot

---

certainty how high the mercury climbs in that region in July; my guess is that it goes completely out of sight!

I toiled and sweated and drank tepid water and chewed Rolaids for about two hours, and I sat in some welcome shade on the flank of an unknown mountain and decided that I would get Carlos to crank up his model A next morning and take me to some more civilized place where I could find an airport or rent a vehicle to take me to Mexico City.

I sat exhausted and very still, feeling my body moisture run down my chest and back. Presently I heard a slight noise. A small bird, I decided, looking towards the sound.

Sitting on its haunches with an amiable and inquisitive look on its face was a spotted cat about the size of a lynx, but sleeker and wearing short, sparse hair. It looked like a small leopard, but lacked the big cat's intensely wild visage. Its face was friendly, almost comical. It could only be an ocelot. We sat and looked at each other for perhaps three minutes, the ocelot relaxed, now and then twitching its slender tail.

I reached for my food satchel, intending to offer to share my lunch with *Felis pardalis,* as the ocelot is known in the scientific world. The cat rose to all fours, stepped back quietly and stopped, undecided whether to stay or go. I found a piece of tortilla and tossed it to the ocelot. It flinched at my sudden movement, but stayed where it was. Then it advanced slowly, smelled the food and looked at me. I am sure it was reproaching me. Casually it turned and walked away, moving in almost total silence.

Because of that cat I stayed my week in the area, and two days later I was lucky enough to spot another one—or maybe it was the same one—from a distance. With field glasses, I watched it for almost half an hour as it hunted for its dinner in broad daylight. Finally it disappeared over a ridge, and that was the end of my observations in the region around Comitan.

Two years later, while in southern Texas, I saw my only jaguarundi as I sat beside a small stream. It came out on the opposite bank and I at first mistook it for an otter. It was otter brown, built low to the ground, and owned an otter-like tail. When it fully emerged through the bank growth and bent to drink, I realized that I was seeing *Felis yaguarundi* for the first time in the wild. The encounter was brief. The cat lapped for perhaps half a minute, looked up, saw me and vanished.

Jaguarundis come in two color phases, red-brown and dark gray. They measure no more than four feet in total length (including tail) and weigh between twelve and twenty pounds. They will hunt night or day, but are more active at night. Any game big enough to subdue is food for the jaguarundi.

The jaguarundi, although the least catlike of all the felines, is quite definitely a cat. It is a secretive animal, moving with great stealth and very shy of man. Little is known about its

habits in the wild. It lives mostly south of the United States border, but some are found in southern Texas.

Ocelots are about the size of a smallish lynx, weighing not more than forty pounds. Their color is variable from buff to grayish, with leopard-like spots on the body, up to the shoulders; dark stripes run from behind the head to the shoulder blades.

Young ocelots generally come in pairs. In Texas, the twins are born during late September or early October in a rocky cave or perhaps in a hollow log. Within a few weeks of birth they go on short hunting trips with the mother or sometimes with both parents, for male and female cats appear to stay together for some time.

Ocelots are, like all cats, meat eaters. They will hunt by day or night and are extremely agile. Any animal large enough to kill is fair game, and where man raises chickens, ocelots can be a problem, for domestic hens are easy to catch and offer great temptation.

These attractive animals are essentially tropical, occurring north of Mexico only in Texas and, rarely, in Arizona. Because they are such friendly creatures, many are kept as pets in the United States and in other parts of the world. It would appear, however, that man's love for ocelots is only skin-deep, as so many have been hunted for their beautiful spotted coats that their continued existence as a wild species may well be in jeopardy.

The Pig that Barks

The peccary is undoubtedly a pig, but it is a strange one compared to the domestic hog. Apart from the fact that it is much smaller, more active, and of a distinctly different color, the peccary can bark, always has twins, lives happily in barren places, and has a musk gland on its back. It is also one of the oldest North American mammals, judging from fossil remains that date back 65 million years.

There is one other distinction that can be claimed by the peccary—it is America's only native pig. From Central and South America, its range extends only slightly into the United States. At one time, about eighty or ninety years ago, it occurred as far north as Arkansas, but unrestricted hunting by man almost brought the species to extinction. Today, with sensible hunting laws in effect, the little pig is more assured of survival and it is fairly plentiful in the southern portions of Texas, Arizona and New Mexico.

A full-grown peccary is about three feet long and stands some twenty-two inches high at the shoulder. It weighs fifty or sixty pounds and has a thick neck, a chunky body with a distinctly arched back, a long snout, and a very short, skinny tail.

On the arch of the back, about eight inches in front of the tail, a musk gland is located deep within the covering of coarse hair. So much like a misplaced navel does this gland appear that one 17th century explorer thought it was indeed just that, and wrote that, if the peccary was killed for meat, it would "so taint all the flesh as not only to render it unfit to be eaten, but make it stink insufferably".

Collared peccary

Certainly, the smell of this musk is offensive to the human nose and it is strong enough to detect from a distance of 200 or 300 feet. Because the pig invariably discharges musk when it is alarmed, it seems obvious that this substance is used as an alarm signal for others of its kind. It may also play a role in breeding, which in the warm climate of their range may occur at any time of year.

The two piglets are born in an underground burrow or inside a hollow log. Although they are only rabbit-sized, young peccaries are able to run and dodge about when only a few hours old. Even at that stage they can move fast enough to keep ahead of a man, though a dog or a wolf could easily catch up to them.

By the time the young are two or three days old, they and their mother leave the nursery area to join a band composed of males, female and young. These bands consist of between five and thirty individuals that scoot through desert mesquite or scrub oak rooting with their long, specialized noses for insect larvae, tubers, toads, lizards, roots, or the eggs of turtles or ground-nesting birds. They love fruit in season, especially the prickly pear which they eat spines and all; manzanita berries are also prized, as are pine nuts, mesquite beans, acorns and catclaw beans. To the peccaries, in fact, all things are food!

Although they can go without drinking for a considerable length of time, they must have water every now and then; and because water is scarce in the semidesert country in which they live, the trails to waterholes are always deeply marked by peccary tracks and around the waterholes themselves the musky scent of these little pigs is almost always evident.

Peccaries are more likely to be heard than seen, for they are wary creatures and generally like to forage or rest within the thick shelter of cactus, mesquite or oak grove. But they do like to talk a good deal and a band's noise is easily audible: grunts, an occasional squeal of rage or pain when a fight develops, guttural snorts and, when alarmed, a sharp but deep note much like a dog's bark, that sends the entire band galloping away as fast as their small legs can take them.

Apart from man, their greatest enemy, peccaries are preyed upon by wolf, ocelot, bobcat, and coyote, but they are not easy animals to subdue and are able to put up fierce resistance, especially when banded for protection. Domestic dogs, of course, will prey on the peccary if they get a chance, but one dog alone is no match for these fierce, agile pigs and even trained hounds are sometimes slashed to death by their sharp canine teeth.

Giant of the Forest

He was taller than a horse and must have weighed three-quarters of a ton. I had never seen anything quite like him before and neither of us knew just what to do about our unexpected meeting on that trail in the north country. He was like a nightmare come true, a giant that towered over me and sprayed in my direction the acrid fumes of his exhaled breath. We stared at each other for perhaps five seconds, then he bolted, leaving me so quickly and quietly that for a moment I doubted whether I had really seen him.

When he was gone the details that had struck my startled senses began to take form in my mind; the humped shoulders and bulbous muzzle, the long stilt-like legs, the dangling "bell" that hung from his throat, and the enormous flattened antlers that grew out of his head like two weird, leafless trees. That was my first mental image of the moose. I had seen pictures of such animals, but I had never before come face to face with one and our brief first meeting created a lasting impression.

The creature was grotesque and terrifying, though he made no threats and, in fact, was probably as afraid of me as I was of him, but a full-grown bull moose, met suddenly within the jungle-like confines of his domain, *is* a frightening sight.

Knowing next to nothing about the world's largest deer, I was not unduly surprised at his sudden appearance (later I came to realize the luck that was with me that evening, for a moose is seldom careless and usually smells or hears an intruder long before he is seen), but the size of the creature amazed me. He must have been seven feet high at the shoul-

Bull moose

der and with his head up and the great antlers above that, some ten feet of moose stood over me and I felt truly insignificant. Fortunately the rutting season—which occurs through October and into November—had not yet affected this particular moose, otherwise the great beast would very likely have charged and at such close quarters I would have been gored to death, for my small-caliber rifle would have done nothing to the brute.

After this meeting I determined to learn all I could of the moose and I spent most of that winter asking questions and scouting the dense forest areas that surrounded my cabin, seeking traces of the beasts, and finding them. One of the first things I discovered about the moose was that despite legs that are over four feet long he seldom leaves the confines of a browse area which generally extends for only six square miles. At first thought this is surprising. Because of his bulk and his capacity for eating one would think that after spending the summer in such a restricted area he would run out of food.

But the moose has a taste for a variety of edibles and the right five or six square miles of bush country can, and does, supply him with all the fodder his big stomach can accommodate, except during times of great cold. He will eat ferns, duckweed, water lilies and their roots, bur-reed, poplar, birch, maple, willow, wild cherry, ash, blueberry, alder, hazel, thimbleberry, honeysuckle and raspberry. In winter he will browse on conifers, if he has nothing else, reaching high up into the trees for the more tender parts. Indeed, without doing more than lift his long neck the moose can reach food growing nine feet from the ground. If he rears on his hind legs he can reach between eleven and twelve feet up and if there is some succulent piece of feeding that is twenty feet above on some sapling, he can generally get it by running his bulbous chin up along the young tree and bringing it down to where his fleshy lips can nibble at it. Sometimes he will straddle a small tree and force his huge body along it, bending it to where he can strip off the leaves, and often snapping the brittle trunk.

He will even pull at grass, a feat more difficult for him than would at first seem possible. His legs were built for browsing or for wading through bogs and shallow lakes, and though rather like a giraffe from the hoofs to the shoulders the moose has not got the giraffe's long neck. As a result he can't reach the ground with his nose unless he bends his front legs and kneels on them, his hindquarters sticking up into the air.

In this attitude he will thrust his neck out, running his chin along the ground, and chop off the grass with his lower cutting teeth. (Like the deer, he has no upper front teeth, but uses his tongue and gums to draw the green food into his mouth, where it is cut off by the bottom teeth.) In this pose he looks silly, especially since he does not move his body but continues the in-and-out motion of his neck and head until he has swept a semicircle clean of grass. Then he will rise stiffly, like an elderly man suffering from rheumatism, and drop down to his knees at another spot.

Cow moose feeding

As a rule the moose minds his own business. His big ears and a keen sense of smell allow him to avoid trouble long before it is near him and he wanders about his territory eating and sleeping and taking frequent baths in lake or pond. He can move quickly when he wants to and he is amazingly quiet about it for an animal that can weigh up to 1500 pounds and is hindered by antlers that can spread for six feet and more. But if he is being chased and is in danger, the moose abandons caution; putting his great head back so the antlers are sloping over his shoulders, their tines pointing in the opposite direction to the one in which he is traveling, he runs, his legs like pistons and his enormous dark body cutting a swath through the bush, and snapped saplings, torn ground and scarred tree-trunks mark his line of travel.

During the rutting season the moose is dangerous. He roams away from his chosen acres and will fight any bull for the favor of a cow. He is always alert and will charge at the sound of an opponent, smashing his way through the forest in a straight line until he sights his rival, then a mighty battle may take place. Usually one of the bulls will break away from the fight, torn and bleeding and perhaps with a broken antler. Now and then the fighters will lock antlers and both may die. Occasionally they are freed by their own efforts, when one of the antlers breaks off, but usually once those great tines lock, they remain that way and the wolves come to claim the fierce bulls.

At mating time the cow moose, which is generally about twenty-five per cent smaller than the bull and has no antlers, becomes noisy and excited. She does a lot of traveling and bellows often, seeking to attract a bull with her hoarse call. At this time she still has last spring's calf with her and the youngster stays with his mother even when the big bull has arrived. The bull will remain with the cow and calf for about nine or ten days, then he leaves to look for another mate and the cow wanders away to browse sleepily in the thickets.

By the end of November the rut is over and the animals have settled again to their various routines. When not eating, which seems to be rarely, they stand and chew the cud, like domestic cattle, perhaps congregating in little bands as the nights grow colder. Such bands usually include two or more cows and their ungainly calves and one or two bulls which have forgotten their rutting season disputes and wander about oblivious of each other.

When winter comes the band of moose can usually be found in some timbered swamp. By now the heavy hair that clothes their bodies the year round has become almost an inch thick; they are in perfect condition, sleek and fat from good summer browsing, ready for the great cold that comes to their dense wilderness. Unless the snow becomes extremely deep the moose do not suffer from it. With their long legs and broad, spreading hoofs they can wander wherever they wish, unhindered by the drifts, but if the winter proves hard and long and much snow clogs their trails they "yard up" at some central point and keep trails open by passing over them daily.

By this time the bull moose has already lost his antlers. These huge racks, which are in their prime during August,

Mother and child

become loose at their base and fall off or are knocked off against some tree. With their loss one would think the bull might feel lightheaded, for the bone head-dress weighs between sixty and eighty pounds. Occasionally I have found discarded antlers lying in some swamp, but more often than not they are eaten that winter by mice, porcupines, rabbits and other creatures, which are seeking the calcium they contain. Often the moose himself will nibble at them, scraping them with his lower teeth.

When winter has gone the moose split up. The bulls are the first to go, seeking a territory for themselves, and the cows begin to look with annoyance on last year's calves. The young moose have grown considerably since their birth and are almost as tall as their mothers, but they are still gangly and untidy-looking and, I believe, quite stupid. For several days the cow tries to discourage the yearling. She lowers her big head and makes running charges at him, which he dodges bleating, and then, probably tired of being a target for his mother's head, the youngster takes the hint and leaves her, a rather pathetic thing as he blunders about the bush, unsure and lonely.

While the yearling is suddenly learning the facts of bush life, his mother is seeking some sheltered spot in which to give birth to her new calf, and the little fellow when born is a strange sight indeed. He looks like his mother, but is a skinny thing, light brownish-red in color, weighing between twenty-five and thirty-five pounds, and he seems to have a lot of trouble untangling his long legs every time he tries to take a step. Usually the calf and the cow spend about three weeks near the birth place, then they roam away, the calf sucking his mother's milk, the cow constantly eating.

They are strange and wonderful animals, these moose, and in many ways are like the wilderness in which they live. They are big and fierce and can kill you if you are unwise in their ways, but they are also graceful and fascinating to watch and will reward one well for the time devoted to their study.

His Last Battle

It was time to die. The elk knew it, and the pines, bulging with fresh snow, looked down and bore witness. The wolf pack surrounded the majestic old bull who stood winded, belly-deep in one of the drifts that blocked the mountain pass. The elk was spent. He had run his final race against the slashing teeth of the timber wolves and now, with indomitable will, he prepared to fight his last battle, resigned to his end, but determined that his hereditary enemies would taste some of the power of his fighting heart.

Old as he was, and tired, the elk would not fall an easy victim to the pack. It was midwinter, and cold. The snow had come early and piled deep this year and famine was about in the mountains, but the elk, a veteran of many such colds, had survived better than most and had lost little of the 1000 pounds that powered his stately shape; and he still had his antlers, great branched weapons that curved over his back and were equipped with long, wickedly pointed tines over his forehead. With these, and his sharp, cloven hoofs, the bull would wage his battle and the thunder of his fight would echo bravely through the green and white vastness of the forested slopes, and his bugling challenge to the pack would ring, albeit for the last time, with regal defiance.

The wolf pack was close on his heels but it stopped when the great elk came to bay. He stood, his legs spread wide, his buff-colored rump close to the bole of a huge pine and his head, bedecked by the magnificent rack, a thing of bristling death. There were seven wolves in the pack and they were led by a big black bitch who was even then advancing slowly towards the elk; the others followed cautiously and soon the seven were ranged in a half-circle around their prey. They sat on their haunches, mouths agape, tongues lolling out, eyes gleaming with the meat lust.

The elk was born in a month of plenty. It was June in the mountains, and the sedges and meadow grasses were abundant when his mother paused in a small thicket of spruces. At first she seemed merely restless, as though she couldn't quite make up her mind to stay there or go on, then the small, bunting life inside her began its journey towards sunlight and a brand new world. He lay where she had dropped him, a tawny bundle, content to stay quiet while his mother's rough tongue stroked the wetness from his matted hair. And when he was dry, showing only an occasional darker patch of dampness on his body, the big cow nudged him with her nose, urging him to his feet. Hunger and his mother's nudgings gave him the vitality to struggle upright, a weaving, trembling little being that stood precariously on rubber legs, but that yet sought and found the full udder with its thick, sweet milk.

Danger lumbered near on the third morning of his life. A matted, shaggy grizzly bear, hungry for meat after a diet of grass and cinquefoil, saw that the mother elk had not gone with the calves and the bulls and the barren cows, but was hanging about in the small mountain meadow, always near the spruce thicket. He watched an entire day and in the evening, while the sun was still suspended over the rimrocks, he trudged down, a savage, shortsighted killer seeking the small bundle of new life that lay still, almost odorless and camouflaged among the scrub that carpeted the thicket floor. The bear, dependent almost entirely on his keen nose and his ears, quartered the area, twice passing within feet of the immobile calf.

On the third trip his line of travel would have taken him right up to the calf, and the cow, who had been watching the lumbering brown bear, charged to the rescue; she bore down on the grizzly, a 600-pound juggernaut who would have run

Elk, bugling

right over the huge bear if he had not swerved from his course. Enraged by the attack, the humpbacked bear tried to reach the speeding cow with a smack from his great paw, but the cow was safely out of reach. The bear shook his head and prepared to continue his search for the calf he was now sure must be near, and the distraught mother stopped and bugled her distress. The call was not as powerful as that uttered by a bull during mating season, but it was nevertheless loud and was heard by other elk mothers in the area. While the cow charged the bear again and yet again, these mothers ran to the rescue.

Cow elk take a great interest in all calves. If a youngster is in need or in danger, and his own mother is not near, any cow in the area will run to his assistance. So it happened this day.

Five shaggy cows trotted into the spruce thicket, and the noise of their coming halted the predator; when he saw them he grunted in anger and turned tail, galloping away from them to seek easier prey elsewhere. The excitement was over for the day and the rescuing cows walked off, some going to their own calves, others stopping nearby to browse on the now succulent feeding offered by the mountains.

The calf lay quiet. He had not moved a muscle during the turmoil. His neck was curled alongside his body, his head up against his rump, and white spots on his flank and on his back blended with the light brown of the rest of him, making him almost invisible where he lay among the sun-dappled shrubs. He weighed almost thirty pounds that day and though his slender bones were still soft, already his body showed something of the majesty it would achieve in the years ahead.

Five weeks passed. The calf, still sucking his mother's milk, was now able to go where she went and, when they were near other elk mothers and their young, to frisk with his small kind. It was now July and the young elk began nibbling on the tender grasses, gradually eating more and more of them. His mother moved away when he tried to suck; only two or three times each day would she let him bunt at her shrinking udders and then for shorter intervals each time, and it did no good for him to bleat his annoyance, for the cow ignored him. In another week his mother would not let him suck at all and after he had spent most of one day trying, he gave up and was content to take his food like the adults.

Feeding time for the elk was during the early morning and in the late afternoon. The days began early, before dawn, and grazing continued for two or three hours. When the sun was quite high, the elk settled in thickets, chewing their cud and looking like rather strange horses with heads and shoulders erect, their front legs curled under and their long back legs stretched out. They stayed that way, generally, until the sun began its downward journey, then they struggled upright and began another feeding session, which would last until the stars winked in the heavens.

The calf grew quickly that summer and by first frost he was almost as tall as his mother and the great antlers with which he would one day do battle showed as two short, blunt knobs. But though he grew big and strong, he was not much to look at that first autumn of his life; he was ungainly, a gangling young fellow who quickly learned to keep away from the breeding bulls during the rutting season, for those monarchs were easily aroused and had little time or patience for a frisking bull calf.

The first snows found the calf tagging at his mother's heels as the herd worked its way down from the high country, southwards, where the valleys were still green and the wind was not so cutting. As they traveled they merged with other elk and the herd numbered almost 300 by the time they reached the winter range, a land of valleys and gently sloping forests in the foothills of the Rockies, where the pines and hemlocks and spruces grew tall and straight, each jostling its neighbor for a chance to reach up and touch the sky.

Here the young bull elk spent the winter. It was cold when the herd arrived and the nights soon grew long. The snow came and the frost crusted the snow so that the elk had to paw through it and nuzzle to reach the wild hay preserved beneath. Though there was food for all, and now and then a warm "chinook" came to help the elk survive, this winter showed the calf something of the intense savagery it could muster. Like the others in the herd, the calf carried cuts on his legs and on his muzzle, where the ice crust had ripped at him when he crashed through to feed.

But the young bull learned many lessons that first winter. He learned to know and to fear man and his rifles, who came soon after the elk reached the low country and for two weeks pursued them and shot many of them; and he learned to fear the fierce timber wolf with its massive jaws and long, rangy legs that could run for hours on end at a speed of twenty miles an hour, not as fast as the elk's best pace, which could top the wolf's lope by ten miles, but persistent and still fresh when the elk had run their last. He learned, too, of the coyotes, the little brush wolves that would not dare attack a healthy elk, but waited until a cripple or a sick animal dropped out of the herd and bogged in the deep snow. And when spring came, he learned his last lesson, which was that he was no longer a calf and that his mother did not want him, for she was going to give birth again.

His life during the next two years was more or less uneventful. Once he was almost run down by a wolf pack; another time he barely escaped a cascade of snow when a loose boulder triggered an avalanche above the trail that led to the old winter range. And many times he fought, mostly in autumn, when the rut was strong on him and his valor greater than his strength and fighting skill. Always he was beaten, for he generally challenged the biggest breeding bull, the animal who had the most cows in his "harem". But the beatings, though painful at the time, were part of his lessons, for after each defeat he escaped a little wiser in the art of in-fighting.

Then came the fourth autumn of his life. He was a massive, healthy young bull then, full of fighting spirit, and already his antlers held some of the stately grace that was to characterize him in the future. He was wandering alone through the high country, alert, pulsing with life, like a prizefighter fresh from training and about to enter the ring. It was late afternoon, but the sun had already hidden behind the peaks, leaving the elk's country in shadow.

A gentle wind fanned the scent of the cows to the young bull. He stopped, wrinkling his nostrils, testing the scent to make sure he was not mistaken. Then he launched his challenge. It was a resonant, clear, bugle call which pealed from him, beginning with a low note, holding for a moment and then rising to a high, stirring contralto which dropped suddenly, paused and became a harsh scream. There was another, almost imperceptible, pause and the scream became a hoarse grunt. Silence enveloped the spruces for the space of ten heartbeats. Then, thrilling and untamed, came the reply to the young bull's challenge; the answer was made less clear by the distance, and perhaps it was a little hoarser, otherwise it might have been a delayed echo of the bull's call.

The elk responded with movement to the unseen bull's acceptance of the challenge. He trotted up the game trail, cleared the spruces and descended into a small alpine valley. A dark bull, his pale rump disc showing clearly in the sunless meadow, presided over twenty cows. He waited for his antagonist on a knoll of ground some fifty yards away from his wives, a fighting machine ready to battle for his harem.

Elk in combat

The young bull walked slowly into the meadow. He stopped, facing his rival as though appraising him, then he charged and the defending bull charged simultaneously. They met head-on, their throbbing necks swollen to almost twice their normal size by the rut, and they wrestled, their antlers rubbing and squeaking against each other, and from the first test of strength the young bull knew this was his day. Slowly he forced the defending bull backwards, closer to the trees, until his enemy broke, wheeled, and fled from the meadow. The fight was over almost before it had started and the young elk had won his first harem.

From that day on he led his cows through the mountains, siring many calves, fighting off challengers and adding to his herd as he went. He grew bigger and his antlers swept back farther and branched out more and he became the king of his mountains. Until one fall day one of his own sons issued a bugle call and the elk answered the challenge and was defeated as his predecessor had been.

Now the elk was going to die. His life had come full cycle and his end was due. That was the law and through that sensitive, infallible instinct all wild things possess, the elk knew this and was ready, being neither afraid of death nor eager for it.

He faced the wolf pack and kept his eye on the black bitch, his great head lowered so that his branching antlers were ready to repel the wolf.

As though at a signal, the whole pack closed in for the kill. Two gray bodies sailed high into the air and landed, bleeding and dead, on the white snow. A third wolf screamed in agony as a long tine pierced his chest.

That was all. The elk was down and the black bitch fastened her curving fangs into his throat and tore the life from him.

He died well, the old bull.

The Swift Ones

The forest floor is a place of many things. Under the crowd-ed balsam firs there is shade and a smooth layer of needles, brown and partly rotted, which does not allow other plant life to take root. The air is cool and slightly moist, and the pupil of the eye must open wide before it can focus on all the indistinct shapes that are here. Beneath the more demand-ing pines there is space, for the root system of these forest giants prohibits other trees from growing near. In some places dappled sunlight filters through and small plants and shrubs, needing less ground in which to set their roots, man-age to establish claim to a few inches of loam. In the heavy shade areas ferns fan out over the ground, giving refuge to small creatures, and near them grow mushrooms of many shapes and hues that offer refreshment to squirrels and chip-munks and birds.

Beyond the pines there is a piece of forest that was once visited by lightning. Three trees have been struck. The an-cient pine was blasted twenty feet from the ground and the spear of fire cleaved through the white, resinous wood, leav-ing a tall stump with a jagged scar that is black on one side and has turned gray-brown on the other; the pine's top sec-tion, sixty feet long, lies rotting on the forest floor, its trunk already hollow, its bark peeling, its regal head just a mass of dry, broken arms. Two big poplars lie dead nearby; the light-ning struck them low down; now short stumps remain, mere shells that are holed by insects. The massive trunks are lying on the floor, moss-covered, pulpy, hosts to ants and wood lice and a million other crawling things. Long grass and golden-

White-tailed deer with fawn

rod grow between the downed trunks and sunlight splashes over them, creating yellow dancing patches that slowly move as the day changes.

Two small animals lie quietly between the poplar trunks, their bodies curled into tight circles, pushed down among the green; they are motionless, silent, and almost without odor, that is why the hunting black bear passed within five feet of them without noticing their presence. The bear's eyes are not so good, but his ears and his nose are sensitive to the slightest sound or smell, yet he passed by these two creatures, fawns of a white-tailed deer.

Four nights ago the bulging doe stopped here and dropped the two little ones; each weighed about four pounds and they were weak and unsteady as the mother licked them dry and nuzzled them into the safety of the grass and ferns. She stayed with them for a time, until they were strong enough to reach for her milk, then, after their meal, she left them

Fawn resting

curled on the ground while she grazed in the forest.

Deer young spend their time alone between feeds for the first two weeks of their life, until they are old enough to follow their mother and start nibbling at young plants. There are two good reasons for this. The mother needs to eat almost constantly if she is to have enough milk to feed her young; and if she stayed near she would quickly lead predators to the fawns.

Alone the little deer stand a much better chance of survival; the meat eaters cannot smell them and nature has colored them so cunningly that they blend with the dappled sunlight pattern of the forest floor; and always the doe knows just where to put her young so that their camouflage will be most effective. Lying flat they are like slight bumps in the terrain. Their hair is reddish-brown, broken by white dots, and this combination creates an illusion of light and shadow even on an overcast day.

When the deer's food supply is good and the does are young and healthy, twin fawns are usually born to them; sometimes, when giving birth for the first time, or if she is very old, a doe may have only one fawn, but at other times three young may be born and four have been known.

The white-tail is a graceful, gentle creature that can fade into its habitat with ghostly stealth, though it may be running at full speed; and it has an unusual system for warning others of its kind that danger is about. Its long tail, brown on top, is snowy white underneath and when the deer is startled it lifts this white flag and holds it up as it runs; the tail is conspicuous then and other deer in the area see it and take warning from it.

An average doe weighs about 120 pounds at maturity and a good buck will scale 200 and even as high as 400 pounds, though this weight is rare. During the summer months the bucks become solitary, staying always in the same area, following the same routes to drink or eat; they are watchful and full of stealth and seem to avoid contact with their fellows.

The does meanwhile are busy with their fawns, trotting over to their hiding places five or six times a day to nurse them and lick them. As soon as the little ones are strong and able to use their slim legs to avoid the many predators that would like to capture them, they follow their mother. Their white spots slowly fade as they grow bigger. By the end of the summer they are colored like the doe, a rich red-brown on the back and sides that fades to cream on the flanks and white on the underparts, and they are almost as big as she is and well able to look after themselves.

The microscopic life that was to be the two fawns began one evening in mid-November of the previous year. This was the time of the rut and the bucks were busy searching for females, their handsome antlers free now of the velvet sheaths that encase the bone when it starts new growth in the spring, and burnished to a gleaming, dark cream color, their

White-tailed deer, buck

points sharp and ready for battle with their opponents. Now and then two bucks meet, and fight. Each regards the other briefly, snorting and pawing. Both charge, meeting on their horns, and the noise of the impact sounds like the cracking of dry sticks. Pushing and shoving, they wrestle until one of them backs off and dashes into the forest, admitting defeat. Often his skin is gashed and streaming with blood from the tines of the victor's head-rack. But sometimes disaster overtakes both fighters; their antlers lock and the bucks then are fated to die of starvation or to fall prey to wolves or other predators.

The mother deer had been feeding in a small clearing since sunset and was almost ready to return to the shelter of the balsams in her forest when a handsome young buck snorted as he emerged into the clearing; the two animals gazed at each other for a few moments; the buck advanced, slowly, lifting his black hoofs high, showing off his great antlers, his swollen neck throbbing with the mating urge. They bred there and stayed together during that night, and in the morning the buck left to seek another doe.

The doe stayed in her territory, feeding on grasses and shrubs, sometimes joining two or three other does for an evening or morning feed, then drifting away; once she met her mate, but she passed him without recognition and he was not interested in her, for she was no longer in heat.

One morning, as the doe was feeding in her small clearing, blue clouds scudded across the sunless sky and a cold, sharp wind began to blow. The deer raised her head and there were bits of grass sticking out from between her lips as she looked to the north. The leaves of the poplars and maples had turned days before. Gradually the green of the maples became yellow and the yellow became mixed with pink and at last a deep, glowing red infused the five-pointed leaves and they began to fall to the forest floor. The poplars meantime became pale; their fresh green was transformed to light yellow and the long-stemmed leaves which shake violently from side to side even in the slightest breeze began to drift down

Deer in winter shelter

also, and this day only a few of the more hardy remained to shiver and shake on the topmost branches.

The doe smelled the air and noticed the change in it. Snow would come before the day was done. She turned away from her feeding and began following a game trail that led to the thick woods, where the balsams hugged each other and sent their branches down to the ground and there was shelter from the cutting winds and good browse in nearby bushes.

That noon the doe stopped to rest in a clump of pines and there were others of her species there; the animals lay on the pine needles, their bodies curled in a nose-to-tail position while the sky grew darker and the wind became stronger and brought the snow, big flakes that were driven by the wind and found their way under the trees. In an hour the forest was white and the recumbent deer were invisible mounds coated by the heavy snow. They stayed that way until the storm passed late that evening, then they struggled stiffly to their feet, shook the snow from their bodies and trotted away, heading for the west and their favorite winter area, a dense cluster of balsams that covered more than one square mile of land. On the way the deer paused to feed, nibbling at the last of the green grasses or raising their heads to pick off the tender shoots of cranberry and willow. They met other deer along the trail; three bucks, their antlers still regal, joined the band, but now there was no enmity between them and they and the does walked on in the darkness, protected from the cold by their new coats, each hair of which is hollow, so that it holds air and offers good insulation.

On the way to their wintering grounds one of the bucks stopped to scratch his head against the bole of a pine; as he rubbed, one of the antlers broke away, leaving a shallow cup on his head where it had been anchored. They went on, the buck looking strange with only one branch left on his head.

Dawn found the deer band almost at their sanctuary, but there was one animal less now. During the night the buck with the one antler had lagged behind, trying to free the other branch from his head, and he had been surprised by three hungry timber wolves. He had tried to run, but the wolves spread about him and one, the leader of the group, lunged at the buck's hindquarters and cut the main tendon to his leg. The buck fell and was torn apart, and the hungry wolves were fed.

January and February passed and the snows piled deep. The deer band numbered eighteen, five bucks and thirteen does; the creatures had yarded in a central area, deep in the heart of the balsam wood. By passing and repassing over their own tracks they kept their trails open as they browsed, reaching ever higher for balsam boughs, daily struggling against the snow to reach a thicket of cedars, a source of favorite winter food. It was a hard winter for the deer.

At last warm winds came and the dead land began to live again. Nine deer survived in the balsam thicket and as the sun drove away the last of the stubborn ice, the creatures, thin and undernourished, left their sanctuary and returned to the mixed forest. The does were big with their fawns and more ragged than the two remaining bucks and they had great need of fresh fodder at this time.

April came and went and so did May and one June morning the doe felt her young become eager for birth. She left the meadow and sought the right place, between the downed logs, and there she dropped her fawns. One was a buck, the other, a little smaller, a doe. Soon they would grow strong and in time they would add new life to the forest, for that is the way of the wilderness.

Herds of the Tundra

Once, several years ago, I went out with a party of scientists on a caribou hunt. We carried no rifles, for our job was not to kill; instead we were "armed" with boats, metal tags and ropes and the object was to find swimming caribou in the James Bay area, rope them, drag them to the side of the boat and tag them before they were released again. All this may sound simple enough, but, of course, it was far from it. Arctic, or barren-ground, caribou weigh between 200 and 700 pounds and their great, branched antlers become a hazard when they protrude over the gunwale of a small boat. We tagged a number of the big deer that day and added a little to the collection of facts relating to the life of these strange beasts.

Naturalists had long been mystified by the caribou's habit of mass migration from one area to another. Many improbable theories had been advanced, but still no one had come up with a reasonable answer. During the 1950s and 1960s, scientists leaned to the belief that food supplies caused the great herds to wander, but this was only theory and more facts were needed before it could be generally accepted. That was why parties of scientists, such as the one I accompanied, were kept busy for several years, tagging and charting the caribou, seeking to discover the secret of their migrations.

Caribou are divided into two species, the barren-ground and the woodland, but it is only the first species that migrates. The woodland caribou, largely because it lives in the

more temperate tree line areas, just wanders wherever the fancy takes it. Physically there is a difference between the two beasts, though it is slight. The woodland caribou is darker and has slightly longer legs; its antlers are more flattened and shorter. It tends to be solitary in the summer and scarcely ever bands into herds larger than six or eight animals until the autumn comes to bring the animals together. During the warm weather the woodland caribou feed much as do the deer, eating early in the morning and in the evening and staying under cover during the hours of daylight.

The barren-ground caribou, however, is a gregarious creature; it likes the company of its own kind and travels about in herds of from twenty to several thousand. Because it lives in a land where night comes hardly at all during the summer, it has become used to eating whenever it is hungry; in fact, it just cannot wait for darkness, or it would starve to death!

Caribou bulls are strange-looking fellows. They are chunky animals, and their hair, when winter prime, is a delicate brown accented by a great white neck ruff that seems to form a beard on the creature's chest. The lower legs, just above the hoofs, are circled with white, and white also runs back from the ruff, over the shoulder and, less distinctly, along the lower flanks. Caribou antlers are different from those of all other deer. Starting with two heavy beams, they fork sharply just above the head; the shorter fork extends forward and downward to the "shovel", a broad, flat tip to the antler that looks rather like the implement which has given it a name; the main branch sweeps back and splits into an array of tines that are flatter and wider than those of the white-tailed deer but not as wide as those of the moose. Unlike any other deer, caribou cows also carry antlers, though these are not nearly as long and handsome as those sported by the bulls; but while the bulls lose their antlers early in the autumn, the females keep theirs through the winter, until May or June, when their calves are born, then they discard them and start all over again, growing new ones.

Throughout the winter both species of caribou look regal in their warm coats, composed, like those of the deer and the moose, of coarse, hollow hairs which are air-filled and give

Barren ground caribou

maximum insulation during the colds of the northland. They are handsome animals then, but by spring, when they begin shedding their winter overcoats, they look ragged and slovenly. Later in the season, a short coat of smooth, dark brown to gray hair replaces the torn winter coat. But because the winter hair comes slowly, hair by hair, the new spring coat does not last long. It looks quite comely at first but it soon begins to change color as each winter hair grows. Handsome in the winter, ugly in the spring, that's the caribou, the black-nosed creature that has baffled science for a good number of years.

When the great autumn migration is on, the caribou swarm over the barrens in their thousands, the noise of their great hoofs, concave and sharp-edged like those of the musk-ox, sounding like the approach of thunder. Another sound accompanies the moving herds. It is a strange, clicking noise, repeated over and over: *click-click-click.* The movements of the

221

ankle bones make the noise, peculiar to caribou, and when thousands of the beasts are walking it is a strange sound indeed.

The vast sea of moving, brown shapes seems to fill the universe; their forked antlers look like a strange, heaving forest that bobs and bends in undulating tempo. Lakes and rivers and streams are forded without hesitation; food is eaten on the run; always the strange beasts seem to be drawn by a magnetic attraction on the far horizon.

That they are seeking fresh supplies of fodder has been proved at last, after many years of patient research. Experience has taught the caribou that when winter comes with its wind-swept, hard-packed snows, they will not be able to reach the lichens which form the greater part of their diet. They know that they must leave the area of crusting snow and find a place where their hoofs and muzzles can reach down and uncover their food supplies. This is why they leave one area and converge on another.

But how do they know what places will soon be covered with hard-packed snow? How do they know that another region will not be mantled in the same way? These are questions that still need answers.

Caribou talk. It may not be a language to human beings, but their rare pig-like grunts constitute a "tongue" of sorts. During the summer, when they are wandering about, these grunts can be heard quite often; but the creatures talk also in sign language, with their heads and antlers and even with their body actions, though only another caribou can understand them.

Summer browse consists of willow leaves, dwarf birches, grass and sedges, but they also eat blueberries, crowberries, Labrador tea, mountain cranberries and horsetail, and of course, they never go by a patch of lichens, their main winter food source, without stopping to nibble. Despite the barren or nearly-barren aspect of the lands upon which they live, they find plenty of food during their erratic wanderings.

By the end of the summer the caribou are fat and in per-

Water is no barrier to the caribou.

fect condition for the hard winter that lies ahead. The bulls, getting ready for the breeding season, have put on extra fat and now their great rumps are covered under the skin with layers of fat that are often three and four inches thick. Late September finds these majestic beasts in the grip of the mating lust; the rut is on, and necks become swollen and tempers begin to fray. Fights break out and those long antlers, clean and shiny and sharp, gouge and rip and thrust during days of bitter quarreling over mates. Like the elk, the bull builds a harem for himself at this time. He dashes here and there, keeping his cows together, collecting other cows or stealing them from a rival, until he has about twelve cows. Finally the rut is at an end and the cold is near. Winter hair is prime; under the hollow guard hairs a layer of fine wool grows for extra protection, and even the black, flaring nose is covered in thick fuzz.

Caribou cows are not prolific. Each has about six calves in her lifetime, which is a wise precaution of nature, for if they produced as many young as other deer the herds would double every three years and would soon eat all the available food supplies. When the young arrive in May or June after a gestation time of 230 days, they are sturdy creatures weighing between eight and ten pounds. Woodland caribou have twins quite often; the barren-ground generally have only one calf. The calves are not spotted like the young of deer and elk, but are a uniform buff-brown color and the lower parts of their legs and muzzles are black.

The Swiftest Ones

A creature that can run at sixty miles an hour, wheel and stop instantly—that's the pronghorn, or prairie antelope, to give it the name by which it is most commonly known.

This dainty, graceful inhabitant of the flatlands has more than a few unusual characteristics, and at least two unique features.

In the first place, the pronghorn is the only native North American hoofed mammal, the *only* one, for the elk, the moose and the deer are immigrants from Europe and Asia via the Bering Strait in Pleistocene times.

But not the pronghorn. It evolved right here. Its ancestry has been traced back some 10 million years, and it has existed in substantially the same form for at least one million. Today this creature has no other living relative in the world, for, although it is called an antelope, it is in no way connected with its namesakes in Africa. That is one of its unique features.

Another is its ability to shed its horn coverings. This sets it aside from all other horned mammals which, once their horn sheath is injured or destroyed, cannot grow a new one.

Perhaps it would be well to explain now the difference between a horn and an antler. Basically, if it is solid it is called an antler; if, on the other hand, it contains a central, pulpy core that is protected by a hard, horny sheath, it is called a horn. Goats, sheep, cows and, of course, prairie antelope, have horns; deer, elk and moose have antlers, and these are shed every year.

But the antelope can shed its horn coverings and does so

Pronghorn antelope

after the rutting season, when the old horn sheaths loosen their grip and eventually fall off. Now the cores of the horns are exposed. Anyone witnessing this transformation for the first time is struck by the shortness of the cores; a buck that may have just shed ten- to twelve-inch horns is seen to have spikes no more than four or five inches long.

The permanent cores of the horns are covered by a thick, softish membrane. Development of the new sheath begins at the tip of the core, extending downwards and, in the case of the buck, also upwards until some four months later they become the classic prongs of the antelope. The doe likewise grows new horn sheaths, but hers are mere short spikes.

As a runner the prairie antelope has few peers, but two other peculiarities of this creature also set it aside from most other mammals. The antelope has two ways of signaling danger to its friends, and both of these are instantly effective.

When alarmed, the twin white disks of hair with which its

buttocks are decorated flare outwards to form conspicuous "powder puffs" that flash a warning to the band. At the same time, from two glands located within the special muscles that erect the white hair, the antelope releases a couple of shots of musk so strong that it can be smelled from 300 or 400 yards away by man and is undoubtedly smelled by other antelope from distances far greater than that. But this is not all! The prairie antelope is a veritable scent factory, having eleven of these musk glands located in different parts of its body. On each back leg, close to the hocks, there is a gland; others are located on either side of the jaw, on either side of the rump, at the base of each horn, and between the claws of the rear hoofs; and there is a single gland on the back. Why so many? We do not yet have the answer to this question, although it is presumed that the scent serves some signal function.

These peculiarities make the pronghorn sound strange, but in fact, standing some three feet at the shoulder and weighing between 100 and 130 pounds, it is a beautiful, graceful animal. It has a tawny body set off by pure white underparts and by the twin white patches on the rump. To accent this striking color combination, it wears nearly-black bands around the throat and on the face. Sleek, glossy, black horns with their distinctive inward-sweeping points complete the picture most readily seen by casual observers. But if you get close enough to an antelope to see its eyes, they surprise you immediately: they are huge, larger than those of a horse, and soft; they shine like black agates and are framed by long black lashes.

Some years ago, in southern Saskatchewan near the Montana border, two buck antelope left their prairie browse to come trotting towards my slowly-moving car. They ran easily, keeping pace with me for a few moments, alongside the car but some ten yards off the highway; then they put on a spurt, passed my car and galloped onto the road. I accelerated from fifteen to thirty-eight miles an hour, but for three miles the antelope kept ahead of me, seeming to be enjoying the game. Then they increased their speed, outdistanced the car and suddenly cut across the highway, streaking away over the prairie. The last I saw of them was when they paused briefly on a knoll and turned to look at me; then they disappeared. It was an impressive sight and an even more impressive display of speed, for I am certain that when they put on their final burst they must have topped fifty miles an hour. Quite likely they would have clocked sixty, had I been able to accelerate in time with them.

This was not my first encounter with the prairie antelope, nor was it my last. But it was the most exciting one, allowing me the chance to see these sleek creatures at close quarters while their lithe bodies were stretched by speed. At the time I had spent almost a year in Saskatchewan, and a good portion of my spare time had been spent watching antelope through field glasses while I lay prone on the prairie, baked by the western sun and gouged by the roughness of native grasses. Once or twice I had been able to coax a band or two within naked-eye view by taking advantage of their curiosity —a habit that got them into serious trouble with the early white hunters of the West, who hunted them nearly out of existence.

In those early days, before the West was opened up, hunters using short-range, low-powered guns could almost invariably lure an antelope into gun-range by lying prone and waving a colored rag slowly back and forth. In doing this they were following the example of Indian hunters, who had used this trick when hunting with bow and arrow. The animals seemed unable to resist such a lure. Today, perhaps because they have been so ruthlessly hunted and because they have become accustomed to the sounds and sights of civilization, it is no longer an easy matter to draw them near. Still, by dint of patient waving, one can eventually attract them close enough for a quick look, although the moment they see the prone outline of a man, or catch his scent, they are off like a flash.

Less than a century ago there were an estimated 60 million antelope on our continent. By 1908 these vast numbers had been reduced to barely 20,000 animals. Since then, strict conservation practices in both Canada and the United States have ensured this graceful creature's survival, but never again will man see huge bands of antelope grazing over the rolling grasslands.

The rutting season for the antelope begins during September or October, at which time the bucks roam around, each seeking to gather a harem of from one to four, or possibly five, does. Now the bucks are proddy, willing to fight a rival on sight. Although these contests are usually of short duration, consisting of quick clashes and a gash or two for the loser, at times a life-and-death fight takes place, when the victor pursues his foe and eventually gores him to death.

Prior to the breeding season the does have spent the summer tending their growing youngsters and have banded with other mothers for protection and company. The bucks have either been alone all summer or have banded with other males to roam the prairie, free from parental responsibility.

Now each buck is busy courting, fighting, and siring next year's young, and for a time the animals are spread in small "marital" groups. Then, the mating time past, the antelope gather in larger bands of 40 to 120 animals. All are in good physical condition; already the winter hair is beginning to grow, replacing the fine summer pelage with hollow, insulating hairs that will keep out the cutting chill of prairie blizzards. It is at this time, too, that both the male and the female begin to grow new horn coverings and lose their old ones.

Food for the antelope means almost anything vegetable that it can graze or browse, depending on the season. In spring it enjoys nibbling on tender grasses and plants and has a special fondness for alfalfa; in winter it must be content with what it can get above the snow. Because of its small hoofs, it does not usually paw for food that is buried under the snow.

Despite the severity of their winter range, the antelope bands survive remarkably well. With the approach of late spring the does begin to think of the new life that they are carrying. Now they feed avidly on the new growth, building their strength and ensuring a supply of milk for the twin fawns that will be born during late May or early June. Old

does, or does who are giving birth for the first time, usually
have only one fawn.

The young are usually dropped wherever the mother happens to be grazing, but some mothers have been known to
select a carefully hidden place in which to deliver their
young.

The babies are light in color, usually fawn or brownish
and, like the fawns of deer, have almost no odor. They lie
immobile, little humps curled on the prairie, dependent for
safety more on stillness and camouflage than on their ability
to run. But run they can, and they have been known to travel
faster than twenty miles an hour just two days after birth.

During their first few days the mother leaves them hidden,
and if she has had twins she places these in different loca-
tions, going round to each one and allowing it to nurse in
turn. Thus, if one of her fawns is discovered by a coyote or a
fox, the chances are that the other will survive.

Once the fawns have "found their feet", they go with their
mother to join a band of other does and their young. Although they still spend a good part of their time lying curled
on the ground, they trot after their mother now and again
and often nurse on the walk.

Now, too, the young antelope become playful, chasing
each other around the adults, building up their leg strength
and their speed; by this time they can usually outdistance an
enemy in a straight run.

Today, when the wolf has been exterminated on the prairies, their biggest natural enemy is the coyote. Foxes will take
some very young fawns, and others may be taken by eagles,
ravens, and bobcats. But predation is not a large factor
in the life of the prairie antelope, whose greatest scourge,
next to man's hunting pressure, is sickness.

Monarch of the Plains

Shaggy beasts move over the great plains. In an unbroken line they stretch from horizon to horizon, a snorting, rumbling wall of living flesh that causes the very earth to tremble, raising from it a pall of dust that obscures the red of an early sun. The thunder of their cloven hoofs dwarfs the noise of the mightiest cataract; the sound made when their short, curved horns crack together is like the breaking of a thousand sticks. They make an incredible roar, an ominous notice of their migration that carries for many leagues over the coarse grass of the prairies.

These are buffalo, the great wild cattle of the western plains, and there are one million of them in this herd, which is just average in numbers during this summer in a time that has gone. Later, when the white man sees them, he will call them after the wild cattle of Africa and Asia; later still, they will be given a name of their own—bison. But this is of no consequence now to the humpbacked giants. They roam unhindered over the flatlands and on this morning in a past age 60 million bison fill the plains.

Imagine, if you can, 60 million mountainous animals cropping at the grass of a plains country so vast it can accommodate them all and yet have enormous areas empty of the cattle-like brutes! Imagine, if you can, a woolly, brown and black bull, weighing 2000 pounds perhaps, standing on a prairie knoll facing into the wind, his massive head hunched, the dark hump atop his great shoulders quivering slightly as he paws at the ground! And there, not many paces away, is the herd, thousands upon thousands of brown shapes as far as the eye can see. The cows, some of them weighing 1000 pounds, the yearlings, and the calves, little yellow-red fellows showing no sign of the hump of their parents, frisking about the old cows. What a spectacle this made, during that summer so long ago!

The herd has stopped. It has spread over the plains and some of the bison are lying down, taking their ease after trotting at about five miles an hour for almost five hours. Here, in the center of the herd, all is quiet. The hungry eat, the tired rest. But out there, out of sight, around the fringes of the herd, only mature bulls are seen and flitting about them, out of reach of the powerful heads with their hooked horns, lurk the wolves, waiting for a sick animal to become separated from his fellows, for a daring calf to leave the side of his mother. And every day the waiting of the meat eaters is rewarded, for in such a herd there are always old and sick animals and many a calf becomes lost.

The history of the buffalo after the white man settled North America is one of tragedy and wanton destruction. In less than two centuries the vast herds were decimated, shrinking from a conservative 60 million animals to a mere handful by the year 1890. Since then, conservationists have managed to rescue the bison from complete oblivion, but they will never be so numerous again. Today there are about 35,000 bison in Canada and the United States.

There is little opportunity for modern animal lovers to study the great buffalo of the plains. True, there are bison in most zoos of the world, but a bison behind bars or wire is not like a herd of his kind roaming free, as the shaggy beasts still do in some of North America's national parks. There, the bison is truly his own lordly self.

The buffalo is gregarious. He loves company and, except for the occasional old bull which age has rendered too bad tempered for tolerance in the herd, these wild cattle roam about in bands, sometimes coming together to form a herd.

Plains bison

Within the band, the old cow, the mother of most of the clan, is the boss, watchdog and general adviser. She is the one that signals danger, and she is the one that generally leads off in search of new grazing areas.

April, May and June are birth months, after the cows have carried their young for nine and a half months, as do domestic cattle. Usually only one calf is born to each cow, though on occasion a cow may have twins. Rarely, a cow may give birth to an albino calf, pure white and entirely or nearly blind.

If grazing has been good, the little ones are allowed by their devoted mothers to nurse well into the winter. At first the youngster looks almost like a farm calf, except that he has a very short neck. But in a few months he begins to look like a buffalo. The bulls start getting their horns two months or so after birth; they are just small bumps high on the forehead, yet, still unlike the powerful weapons they will become when the calves reach adulthood, and the hump that characterizes the buffalo also begins to grow at about this time. By autumn, the young buffalo has shed his reddish fur and has donned his new coat of chocolate brown that is darker about the head and shoulders.

By the next summer the calf has grown enormously. He now has a beard and thick, woolly hair that grows curly on the great head and hangs about his shoulders and down his front legs, ending abruptly almost at the hoofs. In contrast, his low hindquarters and half of his back are sparsely supplied with hair and the flies and mosquitoes find these areas enticing.

It is in order to find relief from the blood-sucking insects that the buffalo rolls in dust or mud. Dropping to his knees, the buffalo heaves his bulk over and over, showing surprising agility for one so big, and continues rolling until he has excavated a wallow that may be ten feet or more across and twelve to twenty inches deep in the middle. Some of these wallows are used again and again by succeeding buffalo and after a rain, when they are filled with water, they become a paradise for some itchy old bull. He will flop into a wallow, roll until his huge body is caked all over with mud, and rumble away from the hole looking as grotesque as any animal can.

Birds are often allies of the buffalo. Blackbirds and cowbirds will often perch on the big back and feed on the bison's tormentors and sometimes numbers of these birds will hop along the ground, at the buffalo's feet, picking up insects. It seems ironical that in winter, when the insects are gone, the buffalo puts on his best, most protective coat and wears it all over his body, and yet there are reasons for this; in the heat of summer he can do without the coat but he must have it to survive at blizzard time.

In it he can stand the fierce prairie winters, which often send the thermometer down to thirty degrees and more below zero. The buffalo, on these days, stands stoically, facing into the wind, perhaps moving in closer to his fellows. In this way he will wait out a blizzard, emerging at the end of the big blow as a shrouded mass of brown and white to trot away and begin clearing the snow with his shaggy head, seeking the natural hay that lies beneath.

From Another Age

Life is a fleeting, insignificant thing on the tundras of the far north. Plains, level and treeless, stretch from one horizon to another, their surface concealed for most of the year by ice and snow. Now and then, to those hardy enough to travel on them, the ice-bound steppes reveal hummocks that were raised in past ages.

Winter on the tundras is a harsh demon that destroys quickly and without mercy; few creatures withstand its attacks. When autumn, with its biting winds and leaden skies, sweeps in on the heels of a brief, bright summer, the herds turn for the south and the tree line and the birds follow overhead. The more solitary animals, like the black bear and the wolf, tough though they are, migrate with the grass eaters, seldom returning to the barrens until the meager sunshine of spring brings new hope to the land.

There is one that stays, though, disdaining shelter: a great, shaggy bovine with curving horns, a hump on its back, and a bad temper. It has the courage and the stamina to survive against the fiercest elements of this wild and lonely land.

It stands, rump turned into the wind, massive head lowered, the long hair that grows over the bony boss of its head hanging like a screen before the small eyes. It is the musk-ox, savage, fearless and hard, the emperor of a land of ice, a relic of prehistory that has survived 20,000 years and more and has seen the death of such legends as the mammoth and the saber-toothed tiger and the woolly rhinoceros. It stands, pawing at its glacial world, a stubborn old warrior that refuses to give up its primitive existence. Its Ice-age contemporaries, un-

Musk-oxen in defensive ring formation

able to adjust to the warming of the earth, slowly perished, but the slow, cumbersome ox looked north and plodded away from the melting glaciers to find his last sanctuary.

The first time I saw a group of musk-ox I became instantly puzzled by the herd's antics. I had left Port Radium, on the eastern shores of Great Bear Lake, as a passenger in an Otter which was heading for Aklavik. The pilot, sighting the beasts before I did, asked if I would like to land and take a look at them. The ski-plane slid to a stop about 300 yards from where the animals had been browsing on scant lichens. They had been startled by the aircraft's engine, but instead of running away, as I thought they must, the oxen bunched in what appeared, even at that distance, to be a circle. I wanted to get out of the plane and walk up close to them, but the pilot refused to let me out.

Musk-oxen are dangerous, I learned, and their strange formation was one of defense, adopted the instant that the shaggy creatures believe they are threatened. In this position, curving, upturned horns facing the enemy, the musk-ox fortress is impregnable. No predator dares the combined might of the oxen, whose young have been pushed into the center of their defensive ring, safe from all but the airborne rifle. When faced by a wolf pack or a polar bear the oxen keep their formation, but they don't rely on defense alone. Now and then one of the big bulls will make a sudden charge, hook at the enemy with his sharp horns and return to the circle. Normally the beasts are slow as they move aimlessly over the tundra, but an enraged bull can charge as swiftly as his distant relative in a Spanish bull ring.

The musk from which these creatures get their name is stored in two glands, one just under each eye, which they rub on their forelegs while they maintain their defensive ring. Though biologists have not yet come up with the complete answer for this action, it is believed the oxen do this to distribute the musk over a wider area, using the scent as well as their fierceness to discourage attackers. Certainly, the musk is pungent and can be smelled by man more than 100 yards away and predators, with their keener noses, may decide that any meal that is as hard to get and smells as bad as the musk-ox is not worth the trouble.

Discounting the long hair and the shape of its horns, the musk-ox is similar to the bison, in profile at least. Its color varies, but is generally dark brown or black, and its hair was designed by the Creator for the cold of its habitat; on the back it is five to six inches long; at the neck, chest and rump it is two to three feet long and hangs straight from the belly and sides, a skirt that reaches to the ankles and at times brushes the ground as the animal walks. On the back, light-colored hair grows in the shape of a riding saddle, its broadest outline over the ribs, extending towards the tail root, its narrow peak stretching to the humped shoulders. Below the hump is a short, strong neck leading to the huge head and those horns which grow out of the boss to the right and left, turn down flatly and then curve upwards again, spreading two feet and more.

Bulls weigh between 500 and 700 pounds, cows between 300 and 500 pounds, but both look heavier; the outer hair is

On the move

bulky enough, but beneath this the animals wear a thick coating of wool. The two coats make the musk-ox look almost twice his size. In the spring the oxen begin to shed their winter hair and then they look ragged and, somehow, more pugnacious. At these times they rub up against any rock or projection they can find and scratch with their hoofs and their horns, seeking to relieve the itch the shedding of their coats creates. It is not uncommon to find hanks of their old hair festooned over the tundra.

Perhaps because they have survived from another age and have faced so many hardships, the musk-oxen have developed a grudge against the world. They keep themselves apart from all others and are quick to anger; a bull snorts once or twice, it lowers its head, wagging it from side to side for a few seconds and then, its small eyes bloodshot, it charges. The bulls are especially proddy during July and August, toward the end of the short arctic summer and just before they begin to seek the cows that will make up their harem.

When two bulls come together in combat the struggle is mightier than that staged by the bison, though the latter are considerably larger and potentially more destructive. The two fighters ram at each other time and again, occasionally cracking their thick, bony frontlets and often killing each other. Frequently their collisions drive both combatants straight up into the air; standing on their hind legs, they pivot like awkward pugilists, which illusion is heightened by the way in which their forelegs strike out at the air. Whereas fights between bison bulls end quickly, the rutting battles of the musk-oxen last considerably longer, and more bulls meet their death on the horns or under the hoofs of their opponents.

When the fight is over, the victor mates with the cow or cows over which he has fought, and by the end of September, just as winter comes to the tundra, the mating season is over. This is the start of real hardship for all the inhabitants of the arctic regions, but the musk-oxen survive, pawing at the snow for frozen plants, turning their broad backs both on the comfort of the south and on the might of the winter storms.

Just as nature has done for the mountain goat, so it has done for the musk-ox. The goat, living in the highest crags, has hoofs that are specialized for its terrain; the musk-ox that lives on the slippery ice of the north has been similarly equipped. The black feet, cloven as in all cattle, have sharp edges that spread wide when weight is put on them; these edges cut into the ice and the result is perfect equilibrium, even when going downhill.

The musk-ox population is not great when compared to the numbers of other wild animals on this great continent, but, while only some 15,000 of the creatures exist in North America today, the species has shown it is able to sustain itself despite the many dangers it has to face. At one time man was responsible for the near-extermination of these wild cattle; white hunters, seeking young calves for the world's zoos, decimated great numbers of the woolly oxen because, to get the calves alive, they had to shoot the adults that formed a defensive ring around them. This has now been stopped. But nature herself maintains a balance of musk-ox population. Be-

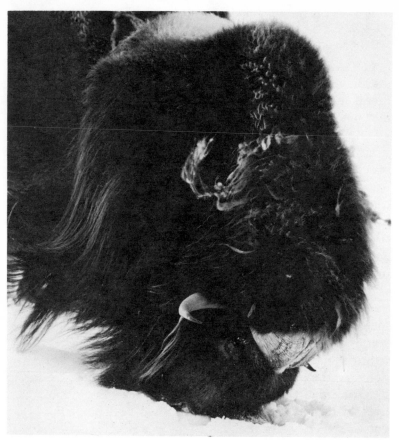

The musk-ox—built for survival

cause of their impregnable defense, few oxen fall prey to carnivores. Two things keep numbers down, however: cows breed usually only every second year; and calves are born during April or May, when the barrens are still tightly gripped by the northland winter, and in the first hours of its life a newborn calf may freeze to death before its birth moisture is dry.

The little fellows weigh between fifteen and twenty-four pounds, and are cloaked in curly brown hair which is about two feet long. During the first ninety days of their life the youngsters live entirely on the milk they receive from their shaggy mothers; after that they go on solid food.

The Lordly Ones

He is the lord of a vast world of crags and glaciers, an agile, sure-footed creature that shuns the warmth and comfort of the lower stretches of land. The bighorn sheep, his massive, curling horns spiraling on either side of his head, stands with hoofs bunched on a peak 7000 feet up, immobile as a statue while he scans the country around him. Below, feeding on a patch of mountain sorrel, are others of his kind; they are all rams, a few old and adorned with great horns, like the big fellow on the rock, others young, some of them last year's lambs, for this is summer and the males are wandering about carefree, in small bands such as this one.

In another part of the mountain range there is a band of ewes and lambs; they are at rest, but one or two of the lambs are frisking, playing tag with each other or bouncing around their mothers. Occasionally one of the little fellows pretends alarm. Bleating mock distress, it dashes to its mother, enjoying a game that may have been ordained by creation, for through this the ewes remain alert and the lambs instinctively learn what to do in the face of danger. Above the resting flock are two ewes, posted on heights as sentinels; they watch for the gliding eagle, or the stealthy cougar, or the lynx, and their keen eyes are constantly scanning the area. When the lambs pretend distress, panic seizes the flock; the sentries have not raised the alarm and the adult sheep cannot understand the danger, and for a while the mothers remain uneasy, fretting and fussy, until the lambs settle to a different game.

Bighorn sheep are majestic creatures. They have the face of their domestic cousins, and similar hoofs and build, but their

legs are longer, their horns are much finer, and they don't carry the curling, thick wool of the domestic sheep. Instead they grow pale brown hair, similar in texture to that of the white-tailed deer, which is tinged with gray on the upper parts of the chunky body; this color varies, as does the coloration of many wild creatures, and can be laced with black or even heavily mixed with dark hair. Seen from the rear, the bighorn's yellow-white rump patch is unmistakable, so are its whitish underparts, doubtless designed by nature to make the sheep hard for predators to see. From below, as it stands on some rocky point, the pale underside blends with its light background, and from above the darker back, neck and head become part of the summer range.

These sheep of the mountains like company, herding in small bands and sticking to a regular schedule of events. At this time of year, when the sun has strength to put some warmth into the peaks, they begin to move in the early morning, while it is still dark, slowly browsing over an area. By the middle of the morning they are satisfied and seek some likely place in which to lie down and chew their cud. Because they eat on the move, they take little time to chew their food, hastily swallowing it and storing it in their rumen, that is, the first section of their four-parted stomach. During the cud-chewing process, they bring up all the food they have swallowed, one mouthful at a time, chew it thoroughly and swallow. It then travels down through the three other parts of the stomach for digestion, and not until the entire meal has been regurgitated and properly chewed do the sheep interrupt their solemn cud ritual.

Shortly after noon bighorns get to their feet and seek a snack; they don't spend much time feeding now, but their empty rumens need something to work on and they eat, go and lie down and begin chewing their cud all over again. A few hours later, when the sun starts its downward journey, they rise once more and have their supper, making a hearty meal this time and probably consuming eight or nine quarts of grass or sedge. By dusk they are ready for bed.

The lordly sheep of the mountains

During the warm weather the ewes have two major pre-occupations, the finding of food and the protection of their young and themselves. Usually each ewe has only one lamb, but twins come quite often. The young ones enter their craggy world in late May or early June while the mother is sheltered in some solitary spot, away from her companions; and this early nursery must be just right. Usually it is at the foot of a cliff or on some high ledge, a place that has only one approach, upon which she can keep a wary eye, for a tender, newborn lamb is eagerly sought by cougars and lynxes and bears.

For a short time the newborn lamb is a helpless little bundle of wetness; its legs seem to be made of rubber; its head appears too heavy for the short neck and wobbles each time it tries to raise it. The mother licks clean her baby, "baaing" softly to it, all the while keeping an extra sharp lookout. But the lamb's helplessness does not last long. An hour or so after its birth it is on its feet and enjoying its first drink of warm milk, still a bit tottery on its spindly legs, but now able to move about under its mother. For a week or so the lamb stays in its nursery each time the ewe goes away to snatch a few hasty bites of food, but after this the little thing goes wherever mother leads and a month later it is a strong, frolicsome creature that must kneel down to suck its mother's milk, for it has almost doubled its size.

Not long after the ewe and her lamb move away from the birth place they are likely to join other mothers and their young and soon a sizable band of ewes and lambs is gathered, each adult taking her turn at sentry duty, all of the ewes alert for danger. Now the lambs are nibbling at young grasses and by fall they are on a full diet of solid food.

The big ram and his bachelor friends have spent the summer together. During this time they got along well, but as November comes and the rutting season nears, they become quarrelsome and now each time they see a ewe they chase her mercilessly, sometimes forcing her to retreat to some narrow ledge where she can fight off their attentions, for the

Rocky Mountain bighorn, a fine old ram

females are not yet ready to breed. The ewes have short,
spike-like horns and they cannot inflict much damage on the
hard-headed rams, but these slight weapons are still enough
to discourage a band of pestering males!

Rams usually gather several ewes into a small harem,
though they do not seem quite as belligerent as elk or caribou and at times will allow a strange ram to approach one of
their wives. Of course, every rutting season there are fights
and the angry rams stand away from each other, rear on their
back legs and charge their opponents, forelegs milling, bodies
almost upright. Crash! The resounding crack of the two great,
horny heads can be heard almost one mile away. After each
charge the rams are dazed for a moment or two, then they
retreat, turn and charge again, until one of the fighters admits

defeat; some battles end in a few minutes, others may last two or three hours, and in the finish the "enemies" may leave the scene of combat as friends, walking side by side as though nothing had happened.

When the rut ends, winter is coming to the mountains. The lambs are almost as tall as their mothers and they are dressed in their new coats; they weigh between seventy and eighty pounds and under the outer coat there is a layer of fine fur. Now the pregnant ewes pay little attention to their offspring and are more concerned with finding enough food in those barren heights to carry them through the winter.

Frozen Peaks

Twin plumes of white vapor spill into the frozen air. They are made by an animal, by the discarded gases from its lungs as they are expelled through black nostrils, and they are seized at once by the pitiless cold and turned into ice dust.

A white goat is breathing. It stands immobile on the icy pinnacle, a sentinel that seems made of the very snow that coats the mountain. Its black horns curve back slightly over its head, its black lips show as a thin line against the whiteness of its coat, and its hoofs, planted firmly at the end of sturdy legs, are like pieces of gleaming ebony. Breath, horns, lips, and hoofs are the only distinct signs made by its body against the blue of the mountain sky.

The creature stares into the distance, its yellow eyes focused on the serried peaks that stretch northward and eventually fade into the mists of the horizon. There is a look of great surprise on the goat's long and solemn face, as though he has just made some sudden and astounding discovery. In reality the goat has discovered nothing at all; he and his kind always look at the world with that amazed expression, produced by a combination of features that characterize this creature of the high mountains. The big, pointed ears, that often stick out at right angles from its head, the rounded forehead, the solemn, staring eyes, the long nose that ends suddenly, as though it has been blunted against some hard object, and the venerable white beard—all these features combine to give the goat his surprised appearance.

In fact, the mountain goat is rarely surprised at anything. And this hardy, courageous beast is not really a goat at all,

Rocky Mountain goat family

his closest relative being the European chamois. However, this white ruminant of the mountains looks more like a goat than anything else, albeit a strange one.

On this day in the subarctic Rocky Mountains the billy goat is, in fact, on sentry duty. Below him, on an area swept clean of snow by the glacial winds, his relatives are browsing on the sparse, dwarf shrubs that grow in stunted disorder on this high rangeland. There is little growing that would sustain life in any other animal, but the white goat of the mountains can get by on scanty food. Today the herd feeds on brush, tomorrow it may move, just a little way, to a patch of mountain sorrel; the next day it may wander a little farther and pull at small clumps of sedges. If it is vegetable and grows on the limited area of their home range, the goats eat it, like it, and thrive on it, no matter how cold the air or how hard the wind blows, for under the long shaggy coats the creatures grow an underfur of fine wool which is often four inches thick and capable of protecting them during any weather.

There are nine goats browsing on the sloping mountain. Three of them are last year's kids, now tough, rangy young-sters almost as big as their mothers. There are two young bil-lies, probably two-year-olds, and there are four nannies, all of which are bulging with the new kids that will be born to them soon, for this is February and the mothers will give birth in May, or perhaps in early June.

Yesterday there were eleven goats in the billy's herd. One, an old, barren nanny, slipped as the billy led them to this place. In her youth, or even one year ago, the nanny would not have fallen, for these mountain dwellers are careful climbers, sure-footed and knowledgeable in the ways of the rocky escarpments upon which they spend most of their lives. But the nanny was old, she was the victim of stomach worms and other parasites, and she was weak and almost blind. She tried to follow the billy, jumped as he did over an area of loose boulders and stumbled on one of them. The path they were following was an almost indiscernible, narrow track that clung to the mountain's edge and the nanny pitched off its surface. The billy and the nine remaining goats stood quietly, watching her gaunt body tumble down the sheer slope, smash against jagged rocks far down and plummet over the rim of a deep canyon. When she had gone the herd resumed its way, uncaring, for the nanny's time had come and she had per-ished.

After eating his fill the billy left the herd and continued climbing, away from the slopes, over crags and steep cliffs un-til he reached the uppermost pinnacle. From here he looked down upon his great, awesome world, secure from his ene-mies and content to stand, statue-like, and chew his cud, now and then moving his strange face to view areas to his left or right. He was a big goat and probably weighed close to 300 pounds: he had massive, heavy shoulders, short legs, and a tail which the Creator must have stuck on to his rump as an afterthought; it was short and stumpy and blended so well with the hairy rump that it was almost invisible.

Movement caught the billy's eye. Below him an indistinct shape appeared to be traveling downhill. The goat stared at it for a moment, then, in order to get a better view, he reared

250

on his haunches, sitting back on them, holding his stubby front legs slightly away from his body. In this position, his round paunch protruding between his bent knees, he stared at the movement and identified it as a free-rolling bush. Satisfied, he returned to his normal stance and continued chewing the cud.

It is late May and the world below the mountains is gay in the trappings of spring. Sunshine floods the valleys and many of the migratory birds have returned and are filling the air with the happiness of their song. The flanks of the mountains are wet with the rushing of streams, though the peaks are still white.

Now there are fifteen goats in the billy's herd. Three of the nannies have given birth, each to one kid; the fourth, a healthy young goat and the last to join the billy's herd, has had two kids. The little ones spent only minutes huddled on the hard earth, then they struggled to their feet and fed from their mothers. Barely one hour later they were prancing and jumping around the older goats, little white things full of bounding energy, their backs made slightly dark by a lacing of brown hair that nature has put there to camouflage them from their great enemy, the high-flying, keen-eyed golden eagle. Lying "frozen" on the ground, the kid's outline with its darker back is hard to see from the air and when the gliding shadow of the eagle is cast over the mountains, only adult goats can be seen moving, for they have nothing to fear from the fierce hunter in the sky.

Five days after the birth of their young the mothers begin to move down the mountain, seeking better pastures for their kids, and soon they join other nannies and their young ones. The billy, meanwhile, has wandered off on his own. Whereas the nannies and the kids will stay in a small area on the mountain's flanks, the billy will roam far, rambling wherever he will, down the slopes, into the valleys and perhaps scaling another mountain.

Ewe and kid

One morning, while he is enjoying the warmth of an early sun, the billy is surprised by two coyotes, big fellows who believe they will feast that day on goat meat. The wild dogs have sneaked towards their prey under the cover of boulders and bushes and now, only twenty feet from the resting goat, they emerge from cover and charge towards him.

The goat cannot outdistance the coyotes and he knows it, but despite their expression of perpetual amazement, mountain goats are not short of courage and the billy is no exception. At his slow pace he cannot escape this fight, so he struggles slowly to his feet, lowers his head and launches his chunky body straight for the nearest coyote, his black, ten-inch horns with their fine points aimed at the wolf's chest.

The two animals meet; the coyote, terrified by the charging goat, tries to swerve from those wicked horns which are even now thrusting upwards, seeking a vital spot. In another moment the coyote rolls backwards, pierced by the horns and too badly injured to scream his agony. The second coyote is almost on top of the goat, but when he sees the havoc the billy has done to his hunting partner he turns away and disappears down-slope.

The billy has become a little more cautious. He leaves the area, peering about for enemies, and travels all the remainder of the morning, stopping only when he reaches the craggy highlands. Here, except for the big cougar and the fierce lynx, the goat is safe and even the cats don't worry him much, for he can go where they can't follow. He travels slowly, but with care and, if he should find himself on some narrow ledge that ends in a sheer drop, though he can't turn around in the normal way, the goat doesn't give way to panic. Instead he lifts his body upright and reaches over his head with his sturdy front legs. His hoofs find purchase on the rock and, like a rather cumbersome ballerina, he turns around, keeping his body close to the rock face, and drops to all fours again, retracing his steps. He can travel over the sheerest rocks without fear of slipping because his hoofs have little concave hollows under them which, when his weight is pressed upon them, act as suction cups.

The billy is a calm, placid fellow and seldom becomes an-

Mountain goat in lordly pose

gry. It is only during the breeding season that his fighting spirit is aroused, but then he can be a very dangerous opponent. This only happens once a year, in November; but even so, many billy goats die on the curved horns of their opponents, fighting for a place beside the nanny of their choice.

After the mating season the goats begin looking for winter quarters, usually halfway up the mountain in areas far enough away from their enemies and high enough for their liking. They move in large herds and sometimes old billies move alone, ignoring their mates.

Photo Credits

Ambler, A. W. (from National Audubon Society), 131
British Columbia Forest Service, 94
Bruemmer, Fred, 110, 219, 223, 236, 238, 240
Claerhout, V., 64, 74 (upper), 233
Coe, D. L. (from National Audubon Society), 137
Crich, R. Victor, 56, 74 (lower)
Dermid, Jack (from National Audubon Society), 12
Gerard, John H. (from National Audubon Society), 165
Goodpaster, Woodrow (from National Audubon Society), 192
Griffiths, Barry, 82, 248
Hall, Tom, 52, 91, 176, 181, 195, 203, 210, 242, 245, 250, 253
Hampson, C. G., 16, 45, 62, 79, 213
Information Canada Photothèque, 107
Lawrence, R. D., 41, 84
Lightfoot, Norman R., 122
Long, Robert J., 77
Montana, State of, 226
Ontario Ministry of Natural Resources, 21, 34, 49, 58, 71, 127, 146, 152, 207, 211
Ott, Charlie (from National Audubon Society), 221
Peck, George K., 189
Quebec Government, 197, 215
Ranford, R. Barry, 30, 199
Reeves, Bucky (from National Audubon Society), 134
Rue, Leonard Lee, III (from National Audubon Society), 68, 116, 139, 168
Scott, Lorne, 100
Staffan, Alvin E. (from National Audubon Society), 25
Van Nostrand, R. (from National Audubon Society), 187
White, Jeanne (from National Audubon Society), 158

Index

Anteater, 29
Antelope, prairie, 225-230
Armadillo, nine-banded, 28-31
Badger, 154
Bats, 23-27
    free-tailed, 26
    guano, 25-26
    leaf-nosed, 26
    little brown, 23-24, 26-27
Bear, black, 116, 119-124, 210
    grizzly, 80, 114-118, 157,
      181, 202-203
    polar, 106-113
Beaver, 54-60, 98, 166
Bees, 123
Bison, American, 231-234
Blackbird, red-winged, 144
Bobcat, 14, 18, 35, 43, 72, 78,
    103, 149, 154, 174-177, 193
Buffalo, 231-234
Cacomixtle, 133
Caribou, 92
    barren-ground, 218-224
    woodland, 218-220, 224
Chickadee, 32, 38
Chipmunk, 47-48, 51-53, 209
Coatimundi, 133
Cougar, 14, 35, 154, 157, 178-184,
    241, 252
Coyote, 14, 18, 73, 78, 93-98, 103,
    140, 172, 193, 230, 252
Deer, 92, 98, 196, 225
    white-tailed, 171-172,
      178-180, 209-217
Dog, 14, 140, 193

Eagle, 73, 78, 103, 154, 175, 230,
    241, 251
Elk, 115, 201-208, 225
Fisher, 35-36, 44, 138-143
Fox, 14, 18, 72, 73, 81, 140, 149,
    154, 171, 172, 230
    red, 99-105
Goat, Rocky Mountain, 247-253
Groundhog, 49, 123
Grouse, 168, 175
Hares, 73, 75, 76-79, 141
    arctic, 76, 78
    snowshoe, 81-87, 169
Jaguarundi, 188, 190
Jay, blue, 38
    gray, 159
Lemmings, 81-87
Lynx, Canada, 18, 35, 60, 72, 81,
    149, 167-173, 252
Marmot, 51, 167-170
Marten, pine, 44, 136-138, 140-143
Mink, 18, 43, 81, 144-149
Mole, common, 19-21
    eastern, 19-21
    hairy-tailed, 22
    shrew, 22
    star-nosed, 21-22
    western, 22
Moose, 92, 194-200, 225
Mouse, 18, 19, 99-101, 123, 141,
    171
    deer, 65
    white-footed, 61-65
Musk-ox, 235-240
Muskrat, 66-72, 145-147, 164

Ocelot, 14, 187-188, 190, 193
Opossum, 11-14
Otter, river, 161-166
Owl, 14, 18, 43, 73, 78, 149, 154
Peccary, collared, 191-193
Pika, 73, 75, 79-80, 171
Porcupine, 32-37, 98, 138-139
Pronghorn, 225-230
Rabbits, 73-75, 141, 175
    black-tailed jack, 78, 79
    eastern cottontail, 74-76
    marsh, 76
    pygmy, 76
    white-tailed jack, 77, 78, 79
Raccoon, 125-129
Ringtail, 130-133
Seal, 106-107, 110-112
Sheep, Rocky Mountain bighorn,
    241-246
Shrew, 141
    long-tailed, 19
    pygmy, 19
    short-tailed, 15-19
    water, 19
Skunk, striped, 150-155
Sloth, tree, 29
Snakes, 78
Squirrel, 98, 172, 209
    black, 39
    flying, 39, 44-45
    gray, 39
    red, 40-44, 136
Trout, rainbow, 161-162
vulture, turkey, 28
Water lily, 144
Weasel, 18, 43, 73, 81

Wolf, brush, 95
    timber, 14, 18, 35, 78,
    88-92, 95, 103, 154,
    156-157, 193, 201-202,
    208, 232
Wolverine, 81, 156-160
Woodchuck, 47-51, 104
Woodpecker, hairy, 38
    pileated, 161